丛书主编　彭新良

The Double Seventh Festival

汉英对照

七夕节

彭新良 谭瑾　编著

陈奇敏　译

阮全友　审校

全国百佳图书出版单位

时代出版传媒股份有限公司

安徽人民出版社

图书在版编目（CIP）数据

七夕节：汉英对照 / 彭新良，谭瑾编著；陈奇敏译 . -- 合肥：安徽人民出版社，2018.8
（多彩中国节丛书 / 彭新良主编）

ISBN 978-7-212-10028-5

Ⅰ.①七… Ⅱ.①彭… ②谭… ③陈… Ⅲ.①节日－风俗习惯－中国－汉、英 Ⅳ.① K892.1

中国版本图书馆 CIP 数据核字 (2018) 第 005208 号

《多彩中国节》丛书

七夕节：汉英对照
QIXI JIE

彭新良　丛书主编
彭新良　谭瑾　编著　　　陈奇敏　译　　　阮全友　审校

出 版 人：徐　敏　　　　　　　选题策划：刘　哲　陈　娟
出版统筹：张　旻　袁小燕　　　责任编辑：陈　娟　周冰倩
责任印制：董　亮　　　　　　　装帧设计：陈　爽　宋文岚

出版发行：时代出版传媒股份有限公司 http://www.press-mart.com
　　　　　安徽人民出版社 http://www.ahpeople.com
地　　址：合肥市政务文化新区翡翠路 1118 号出版传媒广场八楼
邮　　编：230071
电　　话：0551-63533258　0551-63533259（传真）
印　　刷：安徽联众印刷有限公司

开本：880mm×1230mm　1/32　　印张：8.75　　字数：255 千
版次：2018 年 8 月第 1 版　　2018 年 9 月第 1 次印刷

ISBN　978-7-212-10028-5　　　　　　　定价：38.00 元

代　序

我们共同的日子

个人一年一度最重要的日子是生日,大家一年一度最重要的日子是节日。节日是大家共同的日子。

节日是一种纪念日,内涵多种多样。有民族的、国家的、宗教的,比如国庆节、圣诞节等。有某一类人的,如妇女、儿童、劳动者的,这便是妇女节、儿童节、劳动节等。也有与人们的生活生产密切相关的,这类节日历史悠久,很早就形成了一整套人们约定俗成、代代相传的节日习俗,这是一种传统的节日。传统节日也多种多样。中国是一个多民族国家,有 56 个民族,统称中华民族。传统节日有全民族共有的,也有某个民族特有的。比如春节、中秋节、元宵节、端午节、清明节、重阳节等,就为中华民族所共用和共享;世界文化遗产羌年就为羌族独有和独享。各民族这样的节日很多。

传统节日是在漫长的农耕时代形成的。农耕时代生产与生活、人与自然的关系十分密切。人们或为了感恩于大自然的恩赐,或为了庆祝辛勤劳作换来的收获,或为了激发生命的活力,或为了加强人际的亲情,经过长期相互认同,最终约定俗成,渐渐把一年中某一天确定为节日,并创造了十分完整又严格的节俗,如仪式、庆典、规制、禁忌,乃至特定的游艺、装饰与食品,来把节日这天演化成一个独具内涵、迷人的日子。更重要的是,人们在每一个传统的节日里,还把共同的生活理想、人间愿望与审美追求融入节日的内涵与种种仪式中。因此,它是中华民族世间理想与生活愿望极致的表现。可以说,我们的传统——精神文化传统,往往就是依靠这代代相传的一年一度的节日继承下来的。

然而,自从20世纪整个人类进入由农耕文明向工业文明的过渡,农耕时代形成的文化传统开始瓦解。尤其是中国,在近百年由封闭走向开放的过程中,节日文化——特别是城市的节日文化受到现代文明与外来文化的冲击。当下人们已经鲜明地感受到传统节日渐行渐远,并为此产生忧虑。传统节日的淡化必然使其中蕴含的传统精神随之涣散。然而,人们并没有坐等传统的消失,主动和积极地与之应对。这充分显示了当代中国人在文化上的自觉。

近10年,随着中国民间文化遗产抢救工程的全面展开,国家非物质文化遗产名录申报工作的有力推动,传统节日受到关注,一些重要的传统节日被列入了国家文化遗产名录。继而,2006年国家将每年6月的第二个周六确定为"文化遗产日",2007年国务院决定将3个中华民族的重要节日——清明节、端午节和中秋节列为法定放假日。这一重大决定,表现了国家对公众的传统文化生活及其传承的重视与尊重,同时也是保护节日文化遗产十分必要的措施。

节日不放假必然直接消解了节日文化,放假则是恢复节日传统的首要条件。但放假不等于远去的节日立即就会回到身边。节日与假日的不同是因为节日有特定的文化内容与文化形式。那么,重温与恢复已经变得陌生的传统节日习俗则是必不可少的了。

千百年来,我们的祖先从生活的愿望出发,为每一个节日都创造出许许多多美丽又动人的习俗。这种愿望是理想主义的，所以节日习俗是理想的；愿望是情感化的，所以节日习俗也是情感化的；愿望是美好的，所以节日习俗是美的。人们用合家团聚的年夜饭迎接新年；把天上的明月化为手中甜甜的月饼，来象征人间的团圆；在严寒刚刚消退、万物复苏的早春，赶到野外去打扫墓地，告慰亡灵，表达心中的缅怀，同时戴花插柳，踏青春游，亲切地拥抱大地山川……这些诗意化的节日习俗，使我们一代代人的心灵获得了美好的安慰与宁静。

对于少数民族来说，他们特有的节日的意义则更加重要。节日还是他们民族集体记忆的载体、共同精神的依托、个性的表现、民族身份之所在。

谁说传统的习俗过时了？如果我们淡忘了这些习俗，就一定要去重温一下传统。重温不是表象地模仿古人的形式，而是用心去体验传统中的精神与情感。

在历史进程中，习俗是在不断变化的，但民族传统的精神实质不应变。这传统就是对美好生活的不懈追求，对大自然的感恩与敬畏，对家庭团圆与世间和谐永恒的企望。

这便是我们节日的主题，也是这套《多彩中国节》丛书编写的根由与目的。

中国56个民族是一个大家庭，各民族的节日文化异彩纷呈，既有春节、元宵节、中秋节这样多民族共庆的节日，也有泼水节、火把节、那达慕等少数民族特有的节日。这套丛书选取了中国最有代表性的10个传统节日，一节一册，图文并茂，汉英对照，旨在为海内外读者通俗、全面地呈现中国绚丽多彩的节庆文化和民俗文化；放在一起则是中华民族传统节日的一部全书，既有知识性、资料性、工具性，又有可读性和趣味性。10本精致的小册子，以翔实的文献和生动的传说，将每个节日的源起、流布与习俗，图文并茂、有滋有味地娓娓道来，从这些节日的传统中，可以看出中国人的精神追求和文化脉络。这样一套丛书不仅是对我国传统节日的一次总结，也是对传统节日文化富于创意的弘扬。

我读了书稿，心生欣喜，因序之。

冯骥才

（全国政协常委、中国文联原执行副主席）

Preface

Our Common Days

The most important day for a person is his or her birthday while the most important days for all are festivals, which are our common days.

Festivals are embedded with rich connotations for remembering. There're ethnic, national, and religious ones, such as National Day and Christmas Day; festivals for a certain group of people, such as Women's Day, Children's Day, and Laborers' Day; and those closely related to people's life and production, which enjoy a long history and feature a complete set of well-established festive traditions passed on from one generation to another. These are so-called traditional festivals, which vary greatly, too.

China, consisting of 56 nationalities, is a multi-ethnic country. People in China are collectively called the Chinese nation. So it's no wonder that some of the traditional festivals are celebrated by all nationalities while others only by certain nationalities, with the representatives of the former ones being the Spring Festival, the Lantern Festival, the Dragon Boat Festival, the Tomb-Sweeping Festival, and the Double Ninth Festival, etc. and that of the latter being the Qiang New Year, a unique festival for Qiang ethnic group. Each of ethnic groups in China has quite a number of their unique traditional festivals.

The traditional festivals have taken shape in the long agrarian times when people were greatly dependent on nature and when life was closely related to production. People gradually saw eye to eye with each other in the long-term practicing sets of rituals, celebrations, taboos as well as games, embellishments, and foods in a strict way and decided to select some days of one year as festivals with a view to expressing their gratitude to nature, celebrating harvesting, stimulating vitality of life, or strengthening bonds between family members and relatives. In this way, festivals have evolved into charming days with unique connotations. More importantly, people have instilled their common aspirations and aesthetic pursuits into festive connotations and rituals. To put it simply, festivals are consummate demonstrations of Chinese people's worldly aspirations and ideals, and Chinese people's spiritual cultures are inherited for generations by them.

Nevertheless, the cultural traditions formed in the agrarian times began to collapse with human beings being in transition from agrarian civilization to industrial one, esp., in China, whose festive cultures were severely hammered by modern civilization and foreign cultures in nearly one hundred years from being closed to opening up to the world. Nowadays, people strongly feel that traditional festivals are drifting away from their lives and are deeply concerned about it owing to the fact that dilution of traditional festivals means the fall of the traditional spirit of Chinese people. Of course, we don't wait and see; instead, we cope with it in a positive way. This fully displays the contemporary Chinese people's cultural consciousness.

In recent ten years, the traditional festivals have been earning more and more attention and some significant ones are included to the list of the National Heritages with the vigorous promotion of China's Folk Heritage Rescue Program and China's intangible cultural heritage application; for example, China set the second Saturday of June as "Cultural Heritage Day" in 2006; the State Council decided to list three significant traditional festivals as legal holidays—the Tomb-Sweeping Festival, the Dragon Boat Festival, and the Mid-Autumn Festival in 2007. These measures show the state gives priority to and pay tribute to the inheritance of public traditional cultures.

Holidays are necessary for spending festivals which will be diluted otherwise; however, holidays don't necessarily bring back traditional festivals. Since festivals, different from holidays, are equipped with special cultural forms and contents, it's essential to recover those traditional festive customs which have become stranger and stranger to contemporary Chinese people.

In the past thousands of years, our ancestors, starting from their aspirations, created many fine and engaging traditions. These aspirations are ideal, emotional, and beautiful, so are the festival traditions. People usher in the New Year by having the meal together on the New Year's Eve, make moon cakes by imitating the moon in the sky, standing for family reunion, or go to sweep the tombs of ancestors or family members for commemorating or comforting in the early spring when the winter just recedes and everything wakes up while taking spring hiking and enjoying spring scenes by the way. These poetic festive customs greatly comfort souls of people for generations.

As for ethnic minority people, their special festivals mean more to them. The festivals carry the collective memory, common spirit, character of their ethnic groups as well as mark their ethnic identities.

Are the traditional festive customs really out-dated? We're compelled to review them if we really forget them. What matters for review is not imitating the forms of the ancient Chinese people's celebrations but experiencing essence and emotions embedded in them with heart and soul.

Traditions have evolved with history's evolving, but the traditional national spirit has never changed. The spirit lies in people's never-ending pursuit for beautiful life, consistent gratitude and awe for nature, constant aspiration for family reunion and world harmony.

This is also the theme of our festivals and the root-cause of compiling the series.

The Chinese nation, featuring its colorful and varieties of festive cultures, boasts the common festivals celebrated by all nationalities, such as the Spring Festival, the Lantern Festival, the Mid-Autumn Festival, and the ethnic festivals, such as the Water Splashing Festival (Thai people), the Torch Festival (Yi people), Naadam (Mongolian nationality). This series, selecting the most typical ten festivals of China, with each festival being in one volume with figures and in both English and Chinese, unfolds the colorful festive and folk cultures in an engaging and all-round way for appealing to foreign readers. If put together, they constitute a complete set of books on Chinese traditional festivals, being instructive and intriguing. The ten brochures elaborate on the origins, distribution, and customs of each festival in an engaging way with figures, tales, and rich literature. Chinese people's spiritual pursuit and cultural veining can be tracked in this series, serving as a summary of Chinese traditional festivals and innovative promotion of them.

I went over the series with delight, and with delight, wrote the preface, too.

Feng Jicai

CPPCC National Committee member

Former Vice-president of the China Federation of Literary and Art Circles

目　录

多彩中国节

七夕节

Contents

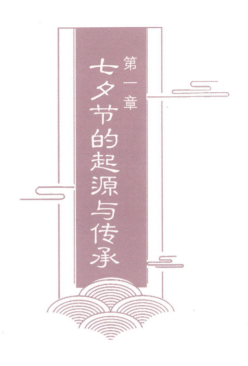

第一章

七夕节的起源与传承

　　在中国，每年农历的七月初七，是传说中的牛郎与织女相会在鹊桥的日子，也是青年男女们重视的日子，因此被称为"中国的情人节"。每当七夕之夜，世间的人们遥望明月寄相思；少女们眼望星空，用彩丝线竞赛穿针乞巧，大显身手，祈求一段美满的姻缘。

一、
七夕节的由来

在中国，农历七月初七这一天是人们俗称的"七夕节"，也有人称之为"乞巧节"、"七桥节"、"女儿节"或"七夕情人节"。这是中国传统节日中最具浪漫色彩的一个节日，也是古代姑娘们最为重视的日子。在这一天的晚上，妇女们穿针乞巧，祈祷福禄寿活动，礼拜七姐，仪式虔诚而隆重；陈列花果女红；青年男女们相约相依，共同赏月，互赠礼物，互诉思念。

（一）七夕节起源的考证

"七夕乞巧"的节日起源于汉代。东晋著名道教学者葛洪在《西京杂记》一书中就有"汉彩女常以七月七日穿七孔针于开襟楼，人俱习之"的记载。一般认为，这是源于古人对自然的崇拜。

"七夕"来源于古人对时间的崇拜。汉语中，"七"与"期"同音，月和日均是"七"，能给人以时间感。古时候，中国人把日、月与金、木、水、火、土等五大行星合在一起，称作"七曜"。七数，在民间表现的是时间的阶段性，人们在计算时间时往往以"七七"为终局。旧时，

人们在给过世之人做道场时，往往以做满"七七"为完满。

"七夕"又是一种数字崇拜现象。中国古代神话说，造物主第一天创造了鸡，第七天创造了人类，所以正月初七又叫"人日"。"七"因此成了与人类生命有关的吉利数字。汉语中，"七"与"吉"谐音，"七七"有双吉之意，表明其为吉利之日。在古代，民间把正月正（春节）、三月三（上巳节）、五月五（端午节）、七月七（七夕节）、九月九（重阳节），再加上预示成双的二月二和六月六，称为"七重"，均被列为吉庆日。汉语中"七"与"妻"同音，于是"七夕"在很大程度上成了与女性相关的节日。

七夕节来源于一种星宿崇拜。古人对神秘的大自然现象无法作出合理的解释，就凭借高超的想象力创造了大量的神话传说故事，对于生活在头顶之上浩瀚无垠的星空也不例外。这种例子是常见的，比如嫦娥奔月的故事。随着天文认识水平的进步，我国古典文献中

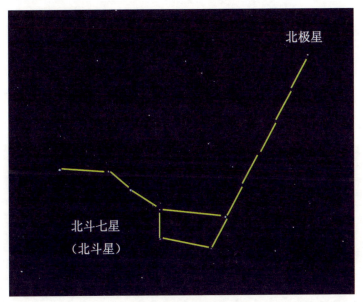

○北斗七星与北极星位置示意图

出现了有关牵牛星、织女星的记载，不仅如此，古人把东西南北各有七颗代表方位的星星合称"二十八宿"，其中以北斗七星最亮，便于夜间辨别方向。北斗七星的第一颗星叫魁星，又称"魁首"。科举制度产生以后，中状元叫"大魁天下士"，读书人称七夕节为"魁星节"，又称"晒书节"。从这里我们可以看到七夕源于星宿崇拜的印记。

多年来，七夕还有一些别的叫法，如"双七"，主要是因为这一天月、日皆为七，也称"重七"。七夕又称"香日"，相传七夕牛郎、织女相会，织女要梳妆打扮、涂脂抹粉，以至满天飘香。七夕还被称为"星期"，牛郎、织女二星所在的方位特别，一年才能一遇，故称这一日为"星期"。唐朝诗人王勃《七夕赋》中的名句"伫灵匹于星期，眷神姿于月夕"，就是把星期与月夕相提并论，点出一年四季中与亲情和爱情相关的最美好、也最凄楚动人的两个夜晚。因此，有人把男女成婚的吉日良辰叫作"星期"。

（二）牛郎织女的早期传说

每年农历七月初七，天气炎热，草木茂盛，天地之间，生机盎然。夜晚，天上繁星闪耀，白茫茫的银河横贯南北。而在银河两岸，各有一颗闪亮的星星遥遥相对，那就是牵牛星和织女星。

牵牛星和织女星因其特殊的位置，留给人无限的遐想。人们给它们起了两个朴实而动人的名字：牛郎和织女。在民间传说中，织女是一个美

○传说中的织女形象

丽聪明、心灵手巧、勤劳而多情的年轻女子，牛郎则是一个朴实勤劳的小伙子。这对被王母娘娘强行分开的夫妻十分恩爱，每年到七月七日这天晚上，就会通过天河上的鹊桥相会。在这个晚上，织女会赐给向她乞巧的凡间女子智慧和巧艺，还能赐给她们美满的姻缘。据说，如果在夜深人静之时，在古井旁，或是葡萄架、瓜架下，听到牛郎、织女隐隐的对谈或是哭泣的声音，就必能得巧。为此，世间不知有多少有女子在这个晚上对着星空祈祷自己能姻缘美满。

直到今日，七夕节仍是我国一个富有浪漫色彩的传统节日，尤其为年轻人所喜爱，但遗憾的是不少习俗活动已弱化或消失，只有象征忠贞爱情的牛郎织女的传说和民间故事广为流传，而"七夕相会"则是传说的经典场景。

追溯七夕节中"牛郎织女"的传说形成过程，时间更要追溯到西周。查经问典，《诗经·小雅·大东》中有"跂彼织女，终日七襄……睆彼牵牛，不以服箱"的诗句。这是一首表现西周时代东方诸侯国臣民怨刺周王室的诗，它的大意是说：银河两岸的织女星、牵牛星，尽管有其名，却不会织布、不能拉车；当今的统治者也是如此，虽身居高位，却无恤民之行，不过徒有其名而已。这里，对织女、牵牛二星仅是作为自然星辰形象引出一种隐喻式的联想，并无任何故事情节。此时，它们只作为一种文化因子，开始进入文学大系统。正是这种"因子"，为后来牛郎织女的传说奠定了人物雏形。

西汉时期，织女、牵牛已被传为两位神人，而且有塑像，面面相对。班固《西都赋》有句："集乎豫章之宇，临乎昆明之池。左牵牛而右织女，似云汉之无涯。"

随着时间的推移，爱情因素与牵牛、织女传说的结合日渐明显。东汉的《风俗通义》中有一段记载："织女七夕当渡河，使鹊为桥，相传七日鹊首无故髡，因为梁以渡织女，故也。"这里的牵牛、织女二星已具人物形象——弄机织布，思念流泪，并且开始被编织为一幕恩爱夫妻饱受隔绝之苦的爱情悲剧。他们每年以喜鹊为桥七夕相会的情节，在民间广为流传，并被融入风俗之中。

三国时期，更有不少诗文反映了这一内容。如曹植《九咏注》说："牵牛为夫，织女为妇，织女、牵牛之星，各处河鼓之旁，七月七日得一会同矣。"可见牵牛、织女已经成为诗人们表现爱恋和思念之苦的一种突出和常用的意象。

二、
七夕节的传说

"两情若是久长时，又岂在朝朝暮暮！"七夕节是一个美丽的节日，是一个让青年男女情愫萌生，让旅人思妇柔肠寸断的日子。这皆因它与一段美丽动人的爱情传说紧密相连——牛郎织女的传说。这个美丽凄婉的爱情故事，千百年来感动了一代又一代的有情人；它已成为我国四大民间爱情传说之一，也是在中国民间流传时间最早、流传地域最广的传说，在中国民间文学史上具有十分重要的地位。

目前，流传至今的牛郎织女传说有很多种版本，但主要是以下两个。

（一）牵牛织女双星下凡

相传，天上有个织女星，还有一个牵牛星。织女和牵牛情投意合，心心相印。可是，天条律令是不允许男欢女爱、私自相恋的。织女是王母的孙女，王母便将牵牛贬下凡尘，令织女不停地织云锦以作惩罚。

织女的工作是用一种神奇的丝在织布机上织出层层叠叠的美丽的云彩，随着时间和季节的不同而变幻它们的颜色，这就是"天衣"。自从牵牛被贬之后，织女常常以泪洗面，愁眉不展地思念牵牛。她坐在织机旁不停地织着美丽的云锦以期博得王母大发慈心，让牵牛早日返回天界。

一天，几个仙女向王母恳求去人间碧莲池一游，王母当日心情正好，便答应了她们。她们见织女终日苦闷，便一起向王母求情让织女共同前往，王母也心疼受惩后的孙女，便令她们速去速归。

话说牵牛被贬之后，落生在一个农民家中，被取名为牛郎。后来父母去世，他便跟着哥嫂度日。哥嫂待牛郎非常刻薄，与他分家，且只分给他一头老牛和一辆破车。

从此，牛郎和老牛相依为命，在荒地上披荆斩棘，耕田种地，盖房造屋。两年后，他们营造了一个小小的家，勉强可以糊口度日。可是，除了那头不会说话的老牛外，冷冷清清的家里只有牛郎一个人，日子过得相当寂寞。牛郎并不知道，那头老牛原是天上的金牛星。

一天，老牛突然开口说话了，它对牛郎说："牛郎，今天你去碧莲池一趟，那儿有些仙女在洗澡，你把那件红色的仙衣藏起来，穿红仙衣的仙女就会成为你的妻子。"牛郎见老牛口吐人言，又奇怪又高兴，便问道："牛大哥，你真会说话吗？你说的是真的吗？"老牛点了点头。牛郎便悄悄躲在碧莲池旁的芦苇丛里，等候仙女们的到来。

不一会儿，仙女们果然翩翩而至，脱下轻罗衣裳，纵身跃入清流。牛郎便从芦苇丛里跑出来，拿走了红色的仙衣。仙女们见有人来了，忙乱地穿上自己的衣裳，像飞鸟般地飞走了，只剩下没有衣服无法逃走的仙女，她正是织女。织女见自己的仙衣被一个小伙子抢走，又羞又急，却又无可奈何。这时，牛郎走上前来，对她说："你若答应做我的妻子，我就还给你衣裳。"织女定睛一看，才知道牛郎是自己日思夜想的牵牛，便含羞答应了他。这样，织女便做了牛郎的妻子。

他们结婚以后，男耕女织，相亲相爱，日子过得非常美满幸福。不久，他们生下了一儿一女，十分可爱。牛郎、织女满以为能够终身相守，白头到老。

可是，王母知道这件事后，勃然大怒，马上派遣天神捉织女回天庭问罪。

这一天，织女正在做饭，下地去的牛郎匆匆赶回，眼睛红肿着告诉织女："牛大哥死了，他临死前说，要我在他死后，将他的牛皮剥下放好，有朝一日，披上它，就可飞上天去。"织女一听，心中纳闷，她明白，老牛就是天上的金牛星，只因替被贬下凡的牵牛说了几句公道话，也被贬下天庭。它怎么会突然死去呢？织女便让牛郎剥下牛皮，好好埋葬了老牛。

正在这时，狂风大作，天兵天将从天而降，不容分说，押解着织女便飞上了天空。

正飞着飞着，织女听到了牛郎的声音："织女，等等我！"织女回头一看，只见牛郎用一对箩筐，挑着两个儿女，披着牛皮赶来了。慢慢地，他们之间

○东莞望牛墩七夕文化节上的牛郎造型

的距离越来越近，织女可
以看清儿女们可爱的模样。
孩子们都张开了双臂，大
声呼叫着"妈妈"，眼看牛
郎和织女就要相逢了。可
就在这时，王母驾着祥云
赶来了，她拔下她头上的

○ 东莞望牛墩七夕文化节上的织女造型

金簪，往他们中间一划，霎时间，一条波涛滚滚的天河横在了织女
和牛郎之间，无法跨越了。

　　织女望着天河对岸的牛郎和儿女们哭得声嘶力竭，牛郎和孩子
们也哭得死去活来。他们的哭声，孩子们一声声"娘"的喊声，是那
样撕心裂肺、催人泪下，连在旁观望的仙女、天神们都觉得心酸难过，
于心不忍。王母见此情此景，也稍稍为牛郎、织女的坚贞爱情所感动，
便同意让牛郎和孩子们留在天上，每年七月七日让他们相会一次。

　　从此，牛郎和他的儿女就隔着一条天河，和织女遥遥相望。在
秋夜天空的繁星当中，我们至今还可以看见银河两边有两颗较大的
星星晶莹地闪烁着，那便是织女星和牵牛星。和牵牛星在一起的还
有两颗小星星，那便是牛郎、织女的一儿一女。

　　到了七月初七那天晚上，成群的喜鹊向着天河扑去，互相咬着
尾巴，搭成一座鹊桥。牛郎一手拉着金哥，一手拉着玉妹上了桥，
织女也从桥那边走到鹊桥中间，一家人相会了。

　　传说，每年的七月七日，若是人们在葡萄架下静静地听，可以
隐隐听到仙乐奏鸣、织女和牛郎在深情地交谈。这一天，姑娘们就
会来到月下，仰望星空，寻找银河两边的牛郎星和织女星，希望能
看到他们一年一度的相会，乞求上天能让自己能像织女那样心灵手
巧，祈祷自己能有如意称心的美满婚姻。由此，形成了七夕节。

○现代舞台演绎牛郎织女鹊桥相会场景

（二）凡间牛郎与天上织女

　　另外一个关于七夕节的传说，也是一则牛郎、织女的凄美爱情故事。

　　传说天帝有七个女儿，她们一起跟王母娘娘学习纺纱织布。很久以前，天空总是碧蓝如洗，没有一丝云彩，天帝觉得这样太单调了，于是吩咐他的七个女儿通过织布给"天"做衣裳。

　　六个姐姐年龄大了，各有各的事儿，虽然天天学，但手艺学得一般。只有最小的妹妹，学习专心，手艺学得特别好。她织出的布，花样多、图案美；她织成的绢，又轻又软。她还能织出层层叠叠的云彩，这些云彩随着时间和节气的变换而变化无穷，其颜色有时洁白如絮，有时红得似火；其形状有时像蘑菇，有时又像各种奇奇怪怪的动物。她给"天"织的衣裳丰富多彩，平时让"天"穿白衣裳，雨天穿灰衣裳，早晨和傍晚穿花衣裳；这些衣裳浑然一体，没有任何缝制的痕迹，被称为"无缝天衣"。王母娘娘见她织布的手艺高，就说："不用给她另外起名字了，就叫她'织女'吧。"从此，人们就叫她织女。

○牛郎的茅草屋微缩模型

织女姊妹七人都长得很漂亮，织女长得最美。织女天天在天宫中坐在织布机前织布。从织女织布机前的窗子往外望，远处有一条闪光的银河。沿着银河往对岸望去，那无所不有的世界就是人间。

人间有一个看牛的牧童，因为他天天牧牛，人们就叫他牛郎。牛郎的父母早已亡故，他跟着哥哥嫂嫂度日。哥哥待他还好，只可惜天天到外面干活，不管家中的事，也管不了家中的事。嫂嫂是个狠心的人，天天逼着牛郎干最重的活儿，只给他吃米糠饼和野菜团子，有时连糠菜都吃不饱。

○湖北省孝感市董永公园里的牛郎织女雕塑

老牛看到牛郎饿得厉害，常常偷偷地流泪。一天，老牛见牛郎饿得走不动了，很心疼他。它想帮牛郎填饱肚皮，就挣脱拴牛绳，到白薯地里去吃白薯藤。它咬着白薯藤，故意用劲往外拽，这样连地下面的白薯就一起拽出。它自己只吃白薯藤，把白薯留给牛郎吃。

牛郎的嫂嫂经常想出许多法儿来虐待牛郎。牛郎也不计较，只是天天到山中牧牛。

有一天，嫂嫂说："牛郎现在已经大了，饭吃得不少，活干得不多，和他分家算了！"哥哥嫂子独占了家里的三间房子、五亩地，牛郎只分到一头老牛。

分家后，没房子住，老牛带着牛郎到一个石洞里住；没地种，老牛帮着牛郎开荒。牛郎在老牛的帮助下，种的庄稼长得特别好，头一年就获得好收成。老牛又帮着牛郎驮来木头、砖瓦，盖起了三间房子。两年后，牛郎家中有吃有住，生活都不用发愁了。

眼看着牛郎到了该娶妻成家的年龄，这一天，老牛忽然说话了。他对牛郎说："牛郎啊，你该成家了。"牛郎叹了一口气，对老牛说道："咱俩是亲密的朋友，你还不知道咱这个家太穷，谁家的姑娘肯嫁我牛郎？"

老牛说："只要你能按照我说的办法去做，就会有姑娘肯嫁给你。天上的仙女，姊妹七人，明天中午就要到银河北面的一个水塘里洗澡。这姊妹七人中，年龄最小的那个，长得最漂亮，心最灵，手最巧，心眼儿也最好。她能纺线，能织布，能做饭，能吃苦。你明天中午先到池塘岸边的树丛后面等着。等她们下水洗澡时，你就把她的衣服拿走。她没有衣服，回不了天宫，就留在人间了。"

牛郎有些犹豫，说："天河是天上和人间的界线，老远就有天兵天将把守，怎么能去得了？"

老牛说："这些你只管放心，到时候你骑在我的背上，我送你去就是了。"

第二天，快到中午的时候，老牛让牛郎坐在它的背上，闭上眼睛，老牛驮着他飞了起来。牛郎闭着眼睛坐在牛背上，只听得两耳生风，一睁眼已经到了银河边。银河很宽，河里的水滔滔滚滚，向着远方流个不停；河水清澈，水面上的水纹在阳光的照耀下，波光粼粼，十分好看。离银河岸边不远，有几个清澈碧绿的池塘。这些池塘远远看去，好像缀在银河带上的颗颗明珠。

过了不久，一群仙女乘风飘然而来。她们长得都很俊美，穿的衣服都很华丽。仙女们在池塘边聚齐了，要到池塘里洗澡的时候，一个仙女说："今天脱衣下水，衣服要按次序放，以免又错穿了衣服。"这样，大姐的衣服放在东边第一棵树下，依次往西排过来，二姐的衣服放在第二棵树下，七妹织女的衣服放在最西边那棵树下。

过了一会儿，池塘里传来了众仙女的说笑声。有的夸水清，有的夸水静，有的嫌水凉，有的怕水深。她们洗得很开心。

牛郎听到众仙女在水中嬉闹，就从树丛后面悄悄地走了出来，来到织女放衣服的树下，拿起织女乘风的仙衣就走。

众仙女洗罢澡，从池塘里出来，各自去穿自己的衣服。织女穿好内衣，要穿那件乘风的外衣，却不见了，四周都找了也没找到。其他仙女怕误了时辰回去要受责罚，都披好乘风衣，凌空而起，飘飘然飞去了，只剩下织女没有仙衣，不能腾云驾雾，回不了天宫。

织女无处可去，猛抬头远远望见牛郎。她走过去问道："这位哥哥，可曾见到我的一件外衣？"牛郎点点头说："见过。"织女请求把衣服还她。牛郎说："我的老牛朋友让我向你提个条件，你肯答应的话，我就还给你。"

织女见这小伙子诚实厚道，话说得朴实、诚恳，相貌端正，体格健壮，心中产生了好感，就问道："有什么条件，你说吧，只要我能办到的，我一定答应。"

牛郎待了好半天，才吞吞吐吐地说出求婚的意思。织女听了，红着脸点了点头。就这样，织女成了牛郎的妻子。

○云南汉服七夕文化节上的牛郎织女表演

牛郎到田间耕田种地，织女在家纺纱织布，夫妇相亲相爱，男耕女织，生活过得幸福美满。弹指过了五年，织女生了两个孩子，一儿一女，都长得伶俐可爱。织女高兴地对牛郎说："人间的生活，自有人间的欢乐。我愿意永远生活在人间，和你白头到老。"牛郎高兴地说："多亏老牛朋友的帮助，咱们才过上幸福的生活。愿咱们永远相爱，永不分离。"

但好景不长。在他们夫妇沉浸在幸福之中的时候，苦难悄悄地降临到他们的头上。天帝和王母娘娘得知织女留在人间嫁给牛郎的消息，大为恼火，立即派遣天兵天将把织女捉回到天廷问罪。王母娘娘怕天兵天将办事粗心，还亲自跟了去观察动静。

这天，牛郎照例到外面去耕地，织女让两个孩子在外面玩耍，自己坐在织布机上织绢。忽然，一群天兵天将闯到织女跟前，不由分说，押解着织女就要返回天廷。织女知道这场灾难躲不过，说道："能不能稍等片刻，让我见一见孩子和孩子的爸爸？"天神哪里肯准，说时间已到，立即押解着织女往回走。

牛郎回到家，见织布机上的布还在机上没织完，织女却不见了，两个孩子在不停地哭。他里里外外找了好几圈也没找到织女。老牛告诉他，天帝知道织女的消息，派天兵天将把她押回天廷去了。

牛郎听说之后，悲痛万分，立刻找了一根扁担、两个箩筐，让两个孩子坐在箩筐里，自己挑着前去追赶。他挑着担子好不容易来到银河，却找不到银河的踪影。原来王母娘娘怕牛郎渡过银河追赶，命令管天河的天神把银河搬到天上去了。牛郎接近不了银河，无法渡河去追赶，只好挑着一双儿女回到家中，再想办法。

牛郎回到家中，孩子哭着要找妈妈。牛郎听到孩子的哭声，撕心裂肺地难过。

老牛见牛郎和两个孩子哭得十分伤心，就说道："牛郎啊，你照顾我多年，如今我已老了，快要死了。我死之后，你把我的皮披在身上，就可以上天去。"

老牛说完话，闭上双眼，死了。牛郎按照老牛说的去做。他披上牛皮，果然能够腾云驾雾。他又挑上儿女，继续去追赶织女。

牛郎升到天空。天空中群星灿烂，他在众星中穿来穿去，追了一程又一程，前面那熟悉的银河已遥遥在望，隔河的织女也仿佛可以望见。牛郎非常高兴，箩筐里的两个孩子也很高兴，伸出小手来招呼妈妈。隔河的织女看见丈夫和两个孩子赶到了，也伸出手来和他们打招呼。

○牛郎挑着箩筐追寻织女

谁知牛郎跑到银河边，正要渡河的时候，忽然有一个无形的东西挡住了他的去路。原来王母娘娘看到牛郎赶来，她怕牛郎赶上会生出许多麻烦，就从头上拔出一根金簪往银河里一划，银河就变成不可逾越的天河。

从此，牛郎只能在天河的这边望着，织女只好在天河的那边招手。他们想彼此倾诉心中的话，但隔得远，听不见。他们想写信，也没法寄递。他们终于想出一个办法：牛郎写好信，捆在牛鞅子上往对方抛；织女写好信，放在织布的梭中，隔河投过去。直到今天，我们在秋夜天空的繁星中间，在那条白练样的天河两边，还可以看到两颗明星，那就是牛郎和织女。牛郎星的前后各有一颗小一点的星，与牛郎星排成一条直线。那两颗小星就是牛郎挑着的两个孩子。离牛郎星稍远一点的地方，有四颗星，排成平行四边形的样子，传说那就是织女抛给牛郎的织布梭。离织女星不远的地方，有三颗星，排成个等腰三角形的模样，传说那就是牛郎抛给织女的牛鞅子。

牛郎、织女就用这种方式传递着他们的思念之情。天河虽然隔断了他们的通路，却隔不断他们真挚的爱情。

牛郎、织女爱得这样深，这样执着，经过多年的努力，终于使天帝稍稍作了一点让步，允许他们每年农历七月七日见一次面。他们的真挚爱情也感动了天宫中的许多姐妹，每年七月七日，各位仙女都主动去送织女渡河；善于传递爱情喜讯的喜鹊也来帮助这一对夫妇在天河上搭桥。牛郎、织女一年相会这一次，见面时彼此诉说着思念之情，说到伤心处，不觉潸然泪下。据说，七月七日这天，人间有些地方会下起阵阵细雨，这雨就是牛郎、织女的泪水。

牛郎织女的故事，在中国很多地方流传的版本都不太一样，但主要情节相似：天上的织女爱上了人间勤劳善良的牛郎，结为夫妻，男耕女织，恩恩爱爱，并生有一对儿女。天上的王母娘娘反对他们的婚姻，用金簪划出天河将他们分开。每年七月七日，牛郎织女相会在鹊桥。

这些传说，都反映了中国古代农业社会底层民众对美好爱情和婚姻自由的向往，是一个中国版的爱情神话。和西方流行的灰姑娘故事模式不同，中国的牛郎织女这种"女强男弱"的配对更容易被歌颂和流传。西方文学中的爱情故事往往是一个贫穷的灰姑娘遇上一个家境富裕的王子，"灰姑娘"碰上了"高富帅"，比如西方童话中的《灰姑娘》；而中国古代的爱情故事都是一个家境富裕的小姐遇到一个家境贫寒或落魄赶考的书生，比如牛郎织女传说、《西厢记》、《牡丹亭》。这也反映出中西方文化差异和民族心理差异，"富贵女嫁贫男"的模式，更加符合封建农耕社会中国劳动人民对神话爱情故事的心理需求，他们（多为中国古代普通阶层的男性）渴望的是仙女下凡与凡人结为夫妻、共同致富，因此也就有了更广泛的群众基础和传播力量。

（三）魁星爷的传说

在中国众多的传说故事中，还有一个与七夕节相关，那就是魁星爷的传说。七夕拜魁星的习俗，来源于这个传说。

相传，七月七日是魁星的诞生之日。魁星是二十八宿中的魁斗星，即北斗七星的第一颗星，它也被称为"魁首"、"文曲星"。因为魁星主掌考运的缘故，所以许多书生都会在魁星生日这一天来拜祭魁星，希望魁星保佑自己多年的辛苦读书生涯能够换来官运亨通。因此，古代学子中状元时被称为"一举夺魁"。

在民间传说中，魁星的童年生活很悲惨，他在襁褓之中时父母便不幸死去了，沦落为一个可怜的孤儿。幸好有一位心地善良、博学多才的先生好心收留了他。魁星非常勤劳、好学，先生很喜欢他，把他视为己出。虽然先生的家庭比较清贫，但是先生从来没有亏待过魁星，不仅为其提供安定的生活，而且还教魁星识字、读书。魁星在先生的悉心教育下，打下了很好的学识基础。但是，魁星长相十分难看，不仅是个跛腿，而且脸上布满麻子，再加上他是个孤儿，因此经常受到同伴们的欺负。每次被人欺负后，魁星都很伤心，这时先生总会安慰他、开导他，教育魁星要把悲愤转化成前进的力量。虽然备受欺负，生活清贫，但是有先生的陪伴，魁星还是比较快乐。

然而，好景不长，在魁星十多岁的时候，先生不幸身染重病，离开了人间。先生临终前，把魁星叫到身边，对他说："我看不到你高中状元了。我死后，你一定要慎思慎行，勤奋学习，坚持理想……"话还没有说完，先生便断气了。先生的离去对魁星的打击很大，他十分伤心，三天三夜没有进食。后来在好心的乡亲们劝慰下，魁星振作精神为先生下葬，而后的三年里，魁星谨记先生临终时的教诲，勤奋读书，废寝忘食。

三年后，魁星在乡试中中了解元。乡亲们、朋友们纷纷来到魁星家为他庆贺。庆贺后，魁星收拾好行李，与乡亲们告别，准备前往京城参加考试。临行前，他来到先生的坟前，挥泪与先生告别。最终，多年的勤奋没有白费，他又高中状元。

魁星喜中状元后，甜甜地进入了梦乡。在梦中，他看到了金銮宝殿，见到了珠光宝气的娘娘，听到了报喜的锣鼓声为他开道，他在人山人海的街道上

○青花瓷观音瓶上的魁星形象

巡游了三天，乡亲们也不远千里来为他祝贺……醒后，他在欣喜的同时，想起了恩重如山的先生，便走到窗前，面对着明月，跪在地上磕头，说："先生的遗嘱，学生一直谨记心中。在今后的仕途中，我也一定会慎思慎行，待日后飞黄腾达，经世济民，回报恩师！"第二天，迎接他的鼓声果真响起。他满腔抱负，来到金銮宝殿，跪着等待娘娘为他戴上簪花。但是这时，不幸的事情发生了——娘娘拿着簪花走到魁星面前时，见魁星相貌奇丑无比，以为是大白天见到鬼了，顿时昏厥在地。皇上见到娘娘被吓昏在地，十分恼怒，命令殿卫将魁星赶出金銮宝殿，并革除了他"三元"的资格。

面对命运的如此捉弄，魁星十分伤心，感叹自己为何如此丑陋。怀着这种羞愧无奈的心情，他回到了家乡。好心的乡亲们知道魁星的悲惨遭遇后，纷纷赶到魁星家，安慰魁星，说："娘娘当时一定是身染疾病，心神恍惚，于是昏厥了。可惜你这样百年不遇的人才了，要怪也只能怪时运不济。没关系，你下次再考，一定会再高中状元的！"在乡亲们的不断劝慰下，魁星逐渐想开了。他感激乡亲们，重新鼓起勇气，又苦读了三年。

三年后，朝廷又举行科举考试。魁星再次收拾行装，离开家乡，来到京城参加考试，最后又高中状元。可是这次在金銮宝殿上，他又把娘娘吓昏了，照样又被驱逐出宫。而后，魁星含恨三年，在得知皇帝已经驾崩，新皇帝的娘娘文武双全、才情过人后，他又满怀希望，参加了考试。可是，不幸的事情再次发生，命运以同样的方式捉弄了魁星，最后他被乱棍赶出宫殿。在一次次的打击下，他精神崩溃了，走路疯疯癫癫，还不停地狂笑，叫喊："鬼，鬼……"突然，他听到乡亲们感叹："太难了！圣上下旨，从今往后开科取士，务必要选择才貌双全的人。可怜魁星，今生今世是不会有机会了！"听到这里，他顿时火冒三丈，仰天长啸："才貌双全？那么，老天啊，你为何要让我生呢？"呼声震彻天地，霎时间电闪雷鸣，狂风大作，暴雨倾泻大地。魁星悲愤地脱下衣冠，赤裸裸地站在雨中，最后跳入东海的巨浪之中。

魁星的自杀惊动了东海龙王。龙王急忙命令龟仙去拯救魁星，于是魁星被救活了。玉皇大帝知道这件事后，被他的悲惨命运和才学感动，赐魁星三元及第，并让他从此掌管人间文事。

因为魁星能左右文人的考运，所以每逢七月七日魁星的生日那天，读书人都郑重地祭拜他，这也成了七夕的一个重要习俗。

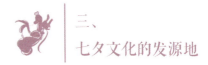

三、七夕文化的发源地

牛郎织女的传说和古老的七夕故事在中华大地广为流传，关于七夕文化的发源地则众说纷纭。一是说牛郎、织女的爱情发轫于"天上银河，地下沂河"的山东省沂源县；二是说在山西省和顺县内有南天池和牛郎峪村，所以有人认为牛郎、织女的"老家"就在那里；三是说牛郎、织女爱情传说的核心区发源于河南省鲁山县，那里至今还流传着很多牛郎织女的后续传说；四是说七夕爱情故事的发源地是湖北省郧西县，"天上银河，地上天河"，天河口有牛郎庙和娘娘山为证；五是说在河南省南阳市有一个牛郎村，在其附近的史洼村又被称为织女村，而村头的小桥更被当地人看做是牛郎、织女约会的地方。

（一）山东沂源：天上银河，地下沂河

牛郎织女的传说始于《诗经 · 小雅 · 大东》中"跂彼织女""睆彼牵牛"的记载。据考证，《诗经》中周王朝的"大东"所描述的地理位置，横跨今山东临淄、曲阜一带，而位于沂河上游的沂源县正介于临淄和曲阜之间，在地理位置上是"大东"的核心地区。

"天上银河，地下沂河"，这是流传于山东省沂源县境内的一种民间通俗说法。"沂河"是发源于山东省沂源县境内的一条全长574千米的河流。"沂河"与"银河"绝妙谐音。目前国内唯一一处以牛郎织女传说为题材的古建筑遗址位于沂源县燕崖乡大贤山上，始建于唐代的织女洞与牛郎庙隔沂河而望。一河两岸的山水格局，与天上"牵牛星－银河－织女星"遥相呼应，有着惊人的相似，形成了天人合一、天地神奇的独特景观。牛郎庙原先是一幢两层阁楼式建筑，后经多次重修，始具规模，建有三间正殿，青砖绿瓦，彩绘斗拱，建筑宏伟。庙内大殿塑有牛郎及其子女像，旁卧金牛塑像一尊。院内古柏参天，清幽别致。

牛郎庙旁边的村庄叫牛郎官庄，村里的人大部分都姓"孙"，与牛郎（孙守义）刚好同姓。这个村子明朝年间就有，村里人以牛郎后代自居，并历代传承牛郎织女故事，至今沿袭着养蚕、织布、取双七水等习俗。

大贤山海拔532米，森林覆盖率96%，悬崖如削，巨石嵯峨，松柏森列，生态环境优良。大贤山下沂河如带，"地上银河"水景长3千米，形成了50多万平方米的水面。

大贤山上，有非常多的石碑，由于年代久远，现存完好的为数

021

不多，但是所有的石碑上所刻的内容，都与牛郎、织女有着或多或少的联系。其中有一块嘉庆二十年（1815年）所立的石碑，上面所刻的两首诗叫《登织女台》，作者是王松亭，诗的第三和第四句"仿佛星河垂碧落，依稀牛女降人间"，对牛郎织女的记载绝美且清晰。

沂源县牛郎织女景区内还有织女泉、织女洞、织女台以及罕见的叶籽银杏、角度不整合面等自然和地质奇观，都与牛郎、织女的传说有关，具有浓重的文化色彩。叶籽银杏是中国独一无二的树种，它所结的果实是长在叶片上的。这里还有一汪清泉，传说是王母娘娘留下的泪珠，被人们津津乐道。在此处，殷红的樱桃也被赋予了一个浪漫的名字，被叫作"爱情果"。

由于各种自然资源与人文脉络高度和谐统一，山东沂源被称为"中国牛郎织女传说之乡"。2008年6月，沂源"牛郎织女传说"被列入第二批国家非物质文化遗产名录。

○沂源县牛郎织女风景区的鹊桥

（二）山西和顺：长期保存七夕文化的民间记忆

山西省晋中市和顺县雄踞太行之巅，位三晋东陲，居两漳之湄。和顺县是国家级贫困县，南天池、牛郎峪一带历来交通闭塞，经济发展滞后，南天池与牛郎峪不到 10 平方千米的境域中保留着与牛郎织女故事相关的自然与人文景观 20 处之多，村民世代传承着生动鲜活的牛郎织女故事和七夕风俗活动，其整体环境与牛郎织女故事的情节十分融洽和谐。

和顺县境内南天池、牛郎峪一带，地处太行山中段，海拔 1800 米的天河梁横亘南北，将南天池村与世隔绝。以天河梁为中心，方圆二十里内，牛郎峪、喜鹊山、南天门、天河池、老牛口等地名与"牛郎织女"故事中的地名对应非常完整，旖旎的自然风光、险峻奇特的山峰和云雾缭绕的山村，恰似天上人间。

和顺县南天池村一带长期保存着关于七夕文化的诸多记忆。民国《和顺县志》记载："七月初七，处女用瓦器生五谷芽，向牛郎织女乞巧。"许多村庄这天讲究吃美食、放鞭炮、贴窗花、敲锣打鼓"接织女回老家"。至今，南天池村仍然保留着七夕"看天"的习俗。

南天池村民讲述的牛郎织女传说与民间流行的故事基本一致，却更加丰富、生动。村民讲，牛郎排行老三，居住在距南天池仅几里路的牛郎峪，其舅姓青名似海，因做食盐生意居南天池村，青似海把织女沐浴的时间地点告诉牛郎，促成了牛郎织女相识相爱；南天池原住户有八姓，为李、乔、张、何、吕、曹等姓，应与"八仙"姓氏相同，王母娘娘派天兵天将下凡抓织女回天宫时，八仙曾经施法阻挡天神，现存的八仙洞、哪吒塔、驴打滚以及托塔李天王放塔之处都与此有关。

每年七月初七夜间，和顺县村民都要在院中南边摆上桌案，供放毛豆（连杆茎煮熟）、玉米（带苞叶煮熟），以及一种被称为"小供"的蒸馍。在这天，当地村民讲究吃好，要放鞭炮、贴窗花（以牛郎织女图案为主）、敲锣打鼓欢庆一番，民间百姓称其为"迎接仙女"或"接织女回老家"。

近年来，和顺县不断挖掘、整理和弘扬牛郎织女文化品牌，并在 2006 年被命名为"中国牛郎织女文化之乡"，"牛郎织女传说"也被国务院正式列为国家级非物质文化遗产。

（三）河南鲁山：牛郎故里，爱情胜地

《鲁山县志》记载："露峰山上有牛郎峒、牛郎庙，民间凡马、牛生病者，祈祷有应。"河南省平顶山市鲁山县辛集乡孙义村一直有关于"牛郎"的原型是该村先祖孙守义的说法。与这个故事相关的地方古迹、自然风物、社会习俗似乎都在为他们的说法提供佐证。

与广为流传的牛郎织女故事不同，在鲁山，还有许多牛郎织女生活的鲜活内容。

据说，织女被抓回天宫，织彩霞云锦，整天闷闷不乐，思念牛郎和儿女。牛郎携儿女在凡间度日，愁苦难言。他们的居住地距鲁山坡顶南天门只有 5 里路，一双儿女在家想念母亲，时不时顺山岭走到南天门要"娘亲"。南天门的把门将军同情他们的遭遇，少不得行个方便，让他们进进出出。玉皇大帝非常喜欢外孙，听任他们来来往往。王母娘娘也放松了对织女的监管，两家的关系也就慢慢融洽起来。牛郎死后被葬于鲁山坡南麓。孙义村牛郎的后裔，则称自己为"牛郎孙"。

后来，牛郎后裔继承了鲁山坡一带家产，并恪守孝道，每年安排腊八、春节、二月八、菜花节、三月三、七夕等十多个节日，请

牛郎织女回村过节。

孙义村旁鲁峰山上的"牛郎洞"、西侧的"九女潭"、山顶的"瑞云观"……似乎都在讲述着牛郎织女动人的故事。

鲁峰山一带自然环境优越，当地百姓自古就养大黄牛。但是与别处养牛不同，辛集乡孙义村虽然家家户户养牛，但养牛不杀牛、牛死后掩埋的习俗一直延续了很久。另外，鲁山自古盛产丝绸，鲁山绸又名"织女织""仙女织"。

如今，辛集乡是远近闻名的葡萄种植基地。这也与牛郎织女故事有关。传说中，牛郎、织女每年七夕相会时，人间的女子在葡萄架下可以听到她们两个人的私语。鲁山民俗"七夕乞巧"，就是在这天向织女乞求赐授巧技，得如意郎君。

在辛集乡，每年的七月初七都会举行大型庙会。经考证，辛集乡的七夕庙会最少有数百年的历史，这一天唱大戏、敲锣鼓、放鞭炮，百姓称其为"迎接仙女"或"接牛郎织女回家"。

鲁山民众千年来坚信牛郎织女是一个真实存在的美好故事，"地上鲁山坡，天上连银河，牛女来相会，人间幸福多"，传唱了千百年的关于牛郎织女的民歌民谣，更是保留了原汁原味的民俗文化，增添了对这一爱情故事的敬仰与缅怀。

2009 年，鲁山县被命名为"中国牛郎织女文化之乡"。此后，鲁山每年都要举办七夕爱情节系列民俗活动，以进一步挖掘鲁山县深厚的牛郎织女文化资源，弘扬民俗文化，彰显鲁山的文化魅力。

（四）湖北郧西：天上银河，地上天河

清代诗人王树德有诗言："群山万壑助讴吟，牵牛天河情更深。细看衣裳飞洒处，站立虹桥忽归林。"这首诗诉说的是牛郎、织女这

○鲁山县举办的七夕节系列民俗活动

一美丽动人、千古流传的爱情传说。诗中提到的"天河"也被说成牛郎织女七夕爱情的发源地。

"天上银河，地上天河。"这是流传于湖北省郧西县境内的一个民间传说。天河是湖北省郧西境内的第三大河流，发源于陕西，全长69千米，流经郧西63千米。天河的西边有三条河，分别是麦裕河（谐音"美女河"）、仙河和归仙河。天河的东北边有一条河叫杨家河。一边是美女仙人，一边是村野俗夫，这就好似一个是天上的仙女，一个是地下的牛郎，他们隔天河相望，诉说着亘古不变的爱情故事。郧西女子的善良美丽、男子的憨厚忠孝、男女之间对爱情的忠贞不渝，无时无处不在印证着这里与古老传说千丝万缕的联系。

归属地之争，湖北郧西极具竞争力。相传，在日本的一本诗集《万叶集》中有牛郎织女的爱情故事发生在中国湖北省十堰市郧西县境内天河的记录。郧西天河名称的来源早已无法追溯，但自古至今从未改过名。郧西的"西"是指方向，郧西应该是牵牛、织女二星神

026

话故事落地的地方。郧西天河不仅在河名上与牛郎、织女故事中的天河重合，而且在天成像，在地成形，在民间成风俗。

在天河口北面山上保留着牛郎庙遗址，至今，这里还流传着牛郎织女的传说。在天河口北面有一座巍峨的娘娘山，传说王母娘娘在此修道成仙，且多次在此召见各路神仙，举办蟠桃盛会，现在山顶还存有娘娘庙、天女下凡古树、八仙石船、蟠桃园、灵宫殿、石林、龙头香等古迹。在天河的上游，两岸有两座遥遥相望的高山，当地人们传说是牛郎山和织女山。在天河中游，城关镇天丰村石门湾的山上，有一具高丈许的石人，状若妇女，人称"石婆婆"；在县城北面的华盖山上有尊石人，状若老头，人称"石公公"。它们被人们称为牛郎、织女的化身。相传，当年牛郎挑着一双儿女追赶织女时，被王母娘娘划天河相隔，牛郎与织女隔河相望，久而久之就形成山峰立在了天河的两岸。郧西古诗词中也记载了天河的美景。七夕的天河之夜，璀璨的星光倒影在江水中，"云影波光乐不眠，一天星斗射江寒。浅斟低唱采莲曲，夜半笙歌出客船"。

湖北省郧西县境内"天河"之名蕴藏着美的传说和美的故事，天河水滋润了美的生态和美的人，天河的自然地貌和人文历史留给了后人承袭美和创造美的基础和空间。种种实物遗存、史料记载、民

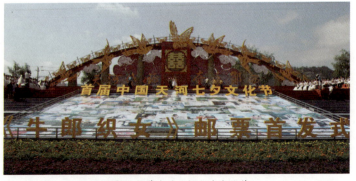

○郧西县举办的天河七夕文化节

间传承等有力的佐证,让地名与传说相对应,湖北郧西因此被誉为"七夕爱情的发源地"。

（五）河南南阳：牛郎织女爱情故事发源地

在距河南省南阳城区西 10 千米左右的国道旁,伫立着一块"牛家宅"村牌。这个只有 300 多人、原本不起眼的小村庄,因为被传是牛郎织女爱情故事的发源地而名动一时。

从牛郎织女的故事,大致可以判断七夕节应源于楚国时期的汉水流域,汉水最大的支流白河环绕南阳城。民俗学家张振犁在《中原古典神话流变论考》中说:"牛郎叫如意,是南阳城西桑林村的人,织女从天上来到人间,与牛郎成亲,亲手教南阳一带的姐妹们学会养蚕,抽丝,织绸缎。"

据生活在这里的老人们回忆,牛家宅旁边曾有一座桥,桥的旁边是一座石碑,石碑的正面刻有一颗牵牛星,牵牛星下面画一头牛,牛前有一人做扬鞭牵牛状,左角有一颗织女星,里面跪坐着一位头挽高髻的女子,两星之间便是天河。而今这块石碑被收藏在河南省南阳市的汉文化馆里。而相距南阳市牛家宅不到 2 千米的史洼村被当地人称为"织女村"。千百年来,史洼村姑娘不嫁牛家宅已成当地民俗。直到今天,史洼村村民也认为,如果把姑娘嫁到牛家宅,就如同七仙女嫁给牛郎,虽然千恩百爱,但是不能长相厮守,白头到老。当地人还把两村之

○河南南阳牛家宅村口的石碑

间的石榴河看做王母娘娘划下的天河。

　　除了以上这些地方，陕西省兴平市、湖北省襄阳市、吉林省长白山地区也都被传为牛郎织女故事的发源地，甚至有媒体报道"各地争夺七夕发源地"。关于牛郎、织女爱情故事的发源地可谓众说纷纭，但是所有这些争论归结于一点，便是当今全中国对传统文化的重视，同时说明了这个美丽的故事流传之广，更印证了人们对美好爱情的不懈追求。

Chapter One

The Origin and Inheritance of Double Seventh Festival

In China, the seventh day of the seventh lunar month is valued greatly by young people and considered as Chinese Valentine's Day, for legend has it that "The Cowherd" and "The Weaving Maid" would meet each other on the Magpie Bridge on that day. That night, Chinese people would gaze at the sky and pin their lovesickness on the distant moon. Girls would show their skills by taking part in the contest of threading needles, and pray to the starry sky for a good marriage.

1. The origin of Double Seventh Festival

The seventh day of the seventh lunar month in China is called "Double Seventh Festival", also known as "Skill Praying Day", "Seven-Bridge Day", "Girls' Day" or "Double Seventh Lover's Day". It is the most romantic one among all Chinese traditional festivals, therefore valued greatly by girls in ancient time. On that night, girls would put flowers, fruits, and needlework on the sacrificial table under the moon, they usually thread the needle to pray for skills, and worship the "Weaving Maid" piously for happiness and longevity. Young boys and girls date in the beautiful moonlight, exchanging gifts and confiding sweetly to each other.

Textual Research on the Origin of Double Seventh Festival

The custom of "praying for skills" on Double Seventh Day began first in the Han Dynasty (206 BC – 220 AD). Ge Hong, a famous Taoist scholar in the Eastern Jin Dynasty (317-420), recorded in Miscellany of the Western Capital that "Palace maids in Han Dynasty often threaded seven-eye needles on the Kaijin Tower on Double Seventh Day, then common people learned to follow the trend."

Textual research shows that Double Seventh Festival originated from ancient peoples' worship for Nature. According the historical records, legends about The Star of Cowherd (i.e. Altair) and The Star of Weaving Maid (i.e. Vega) came into being at least three or four thousand years ago with the development of astronomical knowledge and weaving arts.

Double Seventh Festival also originated from ancient peoples' worship for time and numbers. Since the Chinese character "seven" has the same pronunciation as the Chinese character "period", then if numbers recording the day and the month are both "seven", a glorified sense of time will be aroused. In ancient times, Chinese people named the sun, the moon, the Mercury, the Mars, the Jupiter, the Venus and the Saturn together as "Seven Planets". As seven symbolizes a period of time, people usually use "double sevens" to represent the end of a period. For example, the memorial ceremony held for the deceased used to last for forty-nine days, a "double-seven" complete unit. Seven is also an auspicious number concerning human life. Ancient Chinese myths said that the Creator created chicken in the first day and men in the seventh day, therefore the seventh day of the first lunar month was called the Human Day.

The Chinese character "seven" also pronounces similar to the Chinese character "lucky", so "Double Seventh" stands for double luck, a very auspicious day. Ancient folks chose out "Seven Double Days" from the lunar calendar, namely, the Double First Day, the Double Second Day, the Double Third Day, the Double Fifth Day, the Double Sixth Day, Double Seventh Day and the Double Ninth Day. Then, the number of beads on each line of abacus is strictly seven, presenting a mysterious sense of beauty. Meanwhile, Double Seventh Festival is regarded as a festival of women as well, because of the same pronunciation between the Chinese characters "seven" and "wife".

Some experts hold that Double Seventh Festival comes from people's worship for constellation. Since ancient people cannot give reasonable explanation on mysterious natural phenomena, they created from rich imagination numerous myths and legends, including stories about the vast starry sky. A Typical example is the widespread story of *Chang'e Flying onto the Moon*. With the development of astronomical knowledge, records about The Star of Cowherd (i.e. Altair) and The Star of Weaving Maid (i.e. Vega) appeared in ancient Chinese literatures. Besides, ancient people oriented with the help of each seven stars in the east, west, north or south, which they named " the Twenty-Eight Constellations", and among which the seven stars in the north (i.e. the Big Dipper) are brightest for night walkers to tell the direction. The first star among the Big Dipper was called "The Star of Champion" by ancient Chinese. When the Imperial Examination system was invented in old times, the scholar winning the first place was described as "The champion of all scholars in the world", so Double Seventh Festival was also called "Champion Star Festival" or "Book Airing Festival", a mark of ancient worship for constellation.

There are still other names for the festival in history. For

The Realistic Image of Big Dipper and Polestar

example, some people called it "Fragrant Day", imagining that the Weaving Maid would dress herself up for the meeting with the Cowherd, and her rouge and powder made the sky fragrant. Or the day was named "Stars' Date", for only once in a year could The Star of Cowherd (i.e. Altair) and The Star of Weaving Maid (i.e. Vega) date with each other. "Ode to the Seventh Night", written by Wang Bo the Tang poet, describes lovers "Standing on the Stars' Date, and yearning in the Moon Night", indicating that Double Seventh Festival and Mid-Autumn Festival are two most beautiful and touching nights for Chinese. Therefore, people sometimes call the wedding day "Stars' Date" as well.

Early Folk Legends

It is an enduring Chinese custom to appreciate The Star of Cowherd (i.e. Altair) and The Star of Weaving Maid (i.e. Vega) at the night of Double Seventh Festival.

Every year, the seventh day of the seventh lunar month is beautiful and lively with nice weather and lush plants. At night, the silvery Milky Way bars the starry sky from the south to the north, while two bright stars

The Cowherd and the Weaving Maid in Ancient Chinese Folklore

on the east and west sides of the Milky Way gaze at each other from a distance, being The Star of Cowherd (i.e. Altair) and The Star of Weaving Maid (i.e. Vega).

The special location of Altair and Vega in galaxy aroused rich imagination of people on the earth, who gave the two stars their plain but touching names: the Cowherd and the Weaving Maid. According to folk legends, the Weaving Maid was a clever, beautiful, ingenious girl, while the Cowherd was an honest and hard-working young man. The couple, though loving each other deeply, were forced to separate by the Queen Mother of the West, and were only allowed to meet each other on the seventh night of the seventh lunar month, through the Magpie Bridge over the Heaven River (i.e. Milky Way). On that night, the Weaving Maid would bless girls on the earth who pray for wisdom and handicraft skills, and bestow good marriages to them. It is said that at midnight, usually beside a well or under a grape trellis, if a girl happened to hear the whispering or sobbing of the Cowherd and the Weaving Maid, her wishes surely would come true. Therefore, many girls and young men stay up late that night, praying for a good marriage to the starry sky.

So far, Double Seventh Festival remains a romantic traditional festival, favored especially by young people. Though many traditional celebrating activities have weakened or disappeared, the legends and folk stories on the faithful love between the Cowherd and the Weaving Maid are still wide-spread and influential.

It is definitely not accidental that ancient Chinese chose the seventh day of the seventh lunar month as a festival. Ancient Chinese held a mysterious feeling for the number "seven" out of their worship for time and numbers, and this admiration for "seven" was a cultural phenomenon rather common in the past. "Meeting on Double Seventh Festival" is not included in the plot of initial legend about the Cowherd and the Weaving Maid, but as time goes by, it gradually entered the legend and became a climax of the story.

The legend about the Cowherd and the Weaving Maid related to Double Seventh Festival could be traced back to the Chu State in the Warring States Period (about 476 – 221 B.C.). Among "Minor Odes of the Kingdoms" from The Book of Songs, there is a poem *Large East States* with the earliest record on the story of the Cowherd and the Weaving Maid:

"Three stars make up the Constellation of Weaving Maid;
Seven times a day they are moving.
Bright is the The Star of Cowherd,
But it won't draw our cart."

Another poem from *The Book of Songs*, "The Wide Han River", is also considered as related to the story of the Weaving Maid for the following lines:

"The maiden on the other side of stream
Can but be found in dream."

The "stream" in the poem refers to the Han River, or the Heaven River (i.e. the Milky Way), the "maiden" to the Goddess of Han River, or the Weaving Maid. The people of Chu state lived in the Jianghan region where the Han River flows through, so they attached great importance to the religious ritual for that "Maiden on the other side of stream".

2. Legendary Stories on Double Seventh Festival

"If love between both sides can last for aye,

Why need they stay together night and day?"

Double Seventh Day is a beautiful festival touching the hearts of numerous young men and women, travelers and families. The love story on the Cowherd and the Weaving Maid has moved generations of people and ranked as one the most popular four Chinese folk stories, enjoying an important position in Chinese history of folk literature.

The Star of Cowherd (i.e. Altair) and The Star of Weaving Maid (i.e. Vega) Descending to the World

According to legend, long ago there were two immortals of stars in heaven, namely, the Weaving Maid and the Cowherd. They had deep affection for each other, which is however, forbidden by heaven regulations. Therefore, the Queen Mother of the West banished the Cowherd to the mortal world, while her own granddaughter, the Weaving Maid, must weave brocade of cloud day and night as punishment.

In fact, the work of the Weaving Maid was to weave layers of beautiful clouds with a magic silk, which was called "Heaven Clothes" and able to change colors with the passing moments. After the exile of the Cowherd, the Weaving Maid missed him every day, her face desolate with tearful eyes and frowned brows. She kept weaving beautiful brocade of cloud diligently, hoping the Queen Mother of the West would show mercy and summon the Cowherd back to the heaven.

One day, several fairies requested the Queen Mother of the West for a tour to the Green Lotus Pool in the mortal world, and the Queen Mother gave them consent in a good mood. Seeing the Weaving Maid was gloomy all day long, they continued to ask the permission of the Queen Mother to take the Weaving Maid out together. From an inner fondness for her sad granddaughter, the Queen Mother allowed them to go together on condition that they should return as soon as possible.

Now what happened to the Cowherd after his banishment from the heaven? He lost his immortal being and was born into a peasant's house by chance. When his parents died, he had to live together with his mean brother and sister-in-law. One day, His brother and sister-in-law drove the Cowherd out of home, giving him nothing but an old bull and a shabby cart.

The Cowherd and his bull relied on each other ever since, cultivating the wasteland, plowing the field and building their own house. One or two years later, the Cowherd could manage to lead a simple life in his small home, but he felt so lonely, accompanied only by the bull. The Cowherd had the least idea that the bull is in fact the incarnation of Star of the Gold Bull in heaven.

One day, the bull suddenly spoke to the Cowherd: "Cowherd, go to the Green Lotus Pool today, where some fairies will go bathing. Take away a red dress and hide it, and the fairy owner of the red dress would become your wife." The Cowherd was very surprised to find the bull talk like human, at the same time, he was happy to get the news, so he asked: "Brother Bull, why can you speak like human? And is your word true?" The Bull nodded. Then the Cowherd went to hide in the weed beside the Green Lotus Pool, waiting for the arrival of the fairies.

In no time, the fairies flied down there as expected. They took off their dress and jumped into the pool. At this time, the Cowherd came out and took away the red dress. The fairies saw a man coming out of nowhere, hurrying to put on dresses and flied away. And the only one left behind was the Weaving Maid, who can't find her red dress. Seeing her dress was grabbed away by a young man, the Weaving Maid felt both shy and anxious, losing her idea for the time being. Then, the Cowherd came up to her, asking her to be his wife before returning her dress. When the Weaving Maid looked at the young man carefully, she found that he was actually the Cowherd, the very one she missed day and night. With shyness she said yes to his proposal. Thus the Weaving Maid became the wife of the Cowherd.

After their marriage, the Cowherd and the Weaving Maid love and support each other, leading a very happy life. They gave birth to a lovely boy and a pretty girl, beyond question the happy life in each other's company would last forever.

However, as soon as the Queen Mother got the news, she gave an angry order to capture the Weaving Maid back to heaven immediately.

The Nationally Widespread Legend of the Cowherd and the Weaving Maid

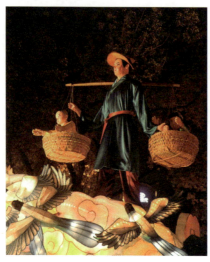

The Model of the Cowherd

That day, when the Weaving Maid was cooking at home, the Cowherd hurried back from the farming field, saying with tears: "Brother Bull died suddenly, and he told me before his death that I should cut off his skin and store it well, because someday I may need to put it on and fly up." The Weaving Maid felt puzzled at the whole matter, as she knew that the bull used to be the Star of Gold Bull in heaven, who got banished for asking mercy for the degraded Cowherd. Why did he die all of a sudden? Anyway, the couple followed the bull's will, skinned him and buried him solemnly.

Just then, gusts of violent wind blew up suddenly and heaven soldiers fell from the sky. They arrested the Weaving Maid and flew up to heaven without giving any explanation.

Being forced to fly back, the Weaving Maid suddenly heard the voice of the Cowherd, "Weaving Maid, wait for me!" Looking back, the Weaving Maid saw the Cowherd flying to her in the bull's skin, a pair of baskets carried on his shoulder, each holding one of their children. The distance between them was shorter and shorter. Now, the Weaving Maid can see her children clearly, and they were opening their arms and calling "Mom" loudly. It was almost the time that the Weaving Maid and the Cowherd could reunite. However, a cloud brought along the Queen Mother then and there, and she pulled off one gold hairpin and drew a line. Instantly, a turbulent heaven river appeared between the two, separating them relentlessly.

Gazing across at her husband and children at the other side of the river, the Weaving Maid cried her heart out, and so is the case with the Cowherd and the two kids. Their heartbreaking crying, mingled with children's calling for mom, touched deeply all the fairies and gods standing by. Even the Mother Queen was somehow moved by their true love, therefore allowed the Cowherd and the children to stay in heaven and to meet with the Weaving Maid once a year on the seventh day of the seventh lunar month.

From then on, the Cowherd and his children lived in heaven, gazing across the heaven river at the Weaving Maid. Now, in starry autumn night, we could recognize two bright stars on two sides of the Milky Way, which are The Star of Cowherd (i.e. Altair) and The Star of Weaving Maid (i.e. Vega). And there are two small stars beside The Star of Cowherd, which are said to be his son and daughter.

On the seventh day of the seventh lunar month when the Cowherd and the Weaving Maid should meet each other, countless magpies would fly up to make a bridge for them. On the Magpie Bridge, the family got their reunion finally! At that moment, the Cowherd and the Weaving Maid looked into each other's eyes lovingly, hugging their children closely, exchanging countless words and endless yearning to each other.

According to legend, on the seventh day of the seventh lunar month each year, if people listen carefully under a grape trellis, they may hear the heaven music from distance and the talking of the Cowherd and the Weaving Maid. As "it is hard to see each other and harder to part from each other", the Cowherd and the Weaving Maid began to count the day for next meeting immediately after their separation.

Henceforth, on the seventh day of the seventh lunar month when the Cowherd and the Weaving Maid meet each other, girls would come out and look up into the starry sky, searching for the two stars divided by the Milky Way, hoping to see the reunion of the couple. They usually prayed to be as skillful in handicraft as the Weaving Maid, and to have a satisfying marriage. The custom promoted the formation of Double Seventh Festival.

The Cowherd and the Weaving Maid

Another legend on Double Seventh Festival tells also a beautiful love story between the Cowherd and the Weaving

The Woodcut on the Cowherd and the Weaving Maid

Maid.

It is said that the Heaven Emperor (i.e. Jade Emperor) had seven daughters, who learnt together from the Queen Mother how to weave. Seeing that the sky was monotonously blue without even a touch of cloud, the Heaven Emperor asked his seven daughters to weave and make "clothes" for the sky.

Unlike her six elder sisters who were distracted to various personal things in daily practice, the youngest daughter was most diligent in learning, therefore most outstanding in weaving skill. She could weave out silk soft and light, cloth with beautiful designs, and layers of cloud with changing colors. These clouds changed colors and shapes with time and season, sometimes white as cotton, sometimes red as fire, sometimes shaping like a mushroom, and sometimes resembling animals. The "clothes" made from her weaving was rich in styles, white for usual days, grey for rainy weather, colorful in the morning and evening. These clothes were praised as "seamless heaven clothes", for they were made as one integrate piece without trace of tailoring. Appreciating her weaving skill greatly, the Queen mother said, "Just call the girl Weaving Maid, which is more suitable than other names." Hence, she was called the Weaving Maid by everyone.

Among the seven daughters, the Weaving Maid is the fairest of the fair. Every day, she sat in the heaven palace weaving, and a look out of her window could reach the shining Silver River in the distance. On the other side of the Silver River was the colorful world where human resided.

In the human world, there is a boy grazing cattle everyday, who was called the Cowherd by people. The Cowherd lost his parents when he was young, and he lived together with his brother and sister-in-law. His brother, though treating him not badly, worked outside everyday and left everything at home to his sister-in-law. And his sister-in-law was not so kind, who forced him to do hardest work and to eat coarsest food, sometimes even starved him.

Seeing the Cowherd was often starving, the old bull shed sad tears. One day, the Cowherd was too hungry to move, the bull felt so sympathetic that it shook off the rope and ran to the sweet potato field, trying to find food for the Cowherd. The bull bit the vine of sweet potatoes and pulled out sweet potatoes from under the field. It ate only the vine part while leaving sweet potatoes to the Cowherd.

The Cowherd was often maltreated by his sister-in-law in different ways, but he didn't complain, just going to the mountain to graze cattle every day.

One day, his sister-in-law said, "The Cowherd has grown up, but he eats much and work little. Let's divide up family property and live apart!" So the Cowherd was given nothing but the old bull, while his brother and sister-in-law took possession of all the houses and farming lands.

Being driven out of home, without shelter or estate, the Cowherd had to live in a stone cave with the old bull, and cultivate new farming land with its help. Under the assistance of the bull, the Cowherd got a good harvest in his first independent year. Then with the log, brick and other materials transported by the bull, he managed to build up a house with three rooms. Two years later, food and living became out of problem for the Cowherd.

Now the Cowherd had grown into a young man and it was time for him to get a wife. One day, the bull suddenly spoke to

him like human: "Cowherd, it's time for you to get married."
The Cowherd answered with a sigh: "We are intimate friends,
and you sure know that I'm too poor to get a wife."

The bull said, "As long as you take my advice, you could
get married. Tomorrow noon, the seven fairies in heaven will
come to have a bath in the pond north of the Silver River. The
youngest among the seven fairies is the prettiest, cleverest and
kindest, who is skillful in weaving and good at cooking, and
most importantly, willing to live a plain life. Tomorrow noon,
you go to hide and wait in the woods beside the pond first.
Seeing them into the pond, you go to take away the youngest
fairy's gown. Without her gown, she couldn't go back to heaven
and have to stay in this world."

The Cowherd asked with some hesitation, "But the Silver
River is the boundary between heaven and earth, with heaven
soldiers guarding there. How could I approach?"

The bull answered, "Don't worry! Tomorrow you can ride
on my back, and I will send you there."

At noon of the next day, the bull let the Cowherd sit on
its back and began to fly. The Cowherd closed his eyes, feeling
wind passing by, and the moment he opened his eyes again he
found himself already on the side of the Silver River. The Silver
River was broad and beautiful, with clean waters shining under
the sunlight, flowing away to the distance. Nearby, there were
several clear green ponds, looking like pearls clung to the belt
of the Silver River from a distant view.

After a while, a group of fairies flew down there, all
beautiful with gorgeous clothes. The fairies stood on the side of
the pond, preparing to have a bath when one fairy said, "Let's
first put in order our clothes today, so we can find them easily

later." Thus, the eldest sister put her clothes under the first tree in the east, the second put hers under the second tree from the east, and accordingly, the youngest fairy put hers under the tree nearest to the west.

Soon, the laughing and chatting were heard from the pond. They bathed happily, making comments on the pond water of that day.

The Cowherd heard the fairies into the pond, walked out of the woods quietly, took away the Weaving Maid's gown and left.

The fairies finished their baths, came out of the pond and went to their own clothes. Then, the Weaving Maid found her outer gown missing. Fearing the punishment for being late, her sisters had to put on their gowns and fly back, with the Weaving Maid left alone, unable to return to the heaven palace without her flying gown.

Helplessly, the Weaving Maid suddenly saw the Cowherd faraway. So she went up to ask, "Excuse me, have you ever seen a gown?" The Cowherd nodded his yes. At the request of the Weaving Maid about returning her gown, the Cowherd said, "Sorry, my bull friend suggested that I should return your gown only on one condition."

Touched by the young man's handsome face, fine figure, honest and sincere look, the Weaving Maid asked, "All right. What's your condition? I'll satisfy it as long as I can."

After quite a while, the Cowherd stumbled out his words of proposal. And, to his joy, the Weaving Maid nodded her consent with a blush.

Thus, the Weaving Maid became the wife of the Cowherd.

The couple led a happy life with the Cowherd working out

in the field, while the Weaving Maid weaving at home. Five years slipping away, the Weaving Maid gave birth to a boy and a girl, both lovely and bright. The Weaving Maid said to the Cowherd gladly, "It's really happy to live in the world. I would like to live here forever, growing old together with you!" The Cowherd answered delightedly, "Thanks to the help of the bull, we could lead such a happy life. I wish we love each other forever, never break up!"

But happy moments always pass by too soon. When the couple were enjoying their life, disaster was approaching them stealthily. Eventually, the news that the Weaving Maid stayed in the mortal world and got married came to the Heaven Emperor and the Queen Mother, who were so outraged that they immediately gave the order to capture the Weaving Maid back to the heaven. Fearing the heaven soldiers were not careful enough to deal with the matter, the Queen Mother went together with the heaven soldiers, making sure nothing was wrong.

That day, the Cowherd went to work in the field as usual, while the Weaving Maid sat before the loom, letting two kids playing outside. All of a sudden, a group of heaven soldiers broke in and took the Weaving Maid away without explanation. Aware that the disaster was unavoidable, the Weaving Maid begged: "Could you please wait for a short while? Let me see my kids and my husband for the last time!" But the heaven soldiers would not allow, just saying the time was up and arresting her away instantly.

When the Cowherd came back, he found the cloth was half-finished on the loom and the kids were crying loudly, yet the Weaving Maid was nowhere around. The old bull told him that his wife had been caught back to the heaven by heaven soldiers from the order of the Heaven Emperor.

The Cowherd was so sad at the news, and he ran to chase after his wife at once, with two kids carried in two baskets on a shoulder pole. Through all difficulties he arrived at the place where used to be the Silver River, but no trace of river could be found now. Actually, the Queen Mother had ordered a god to move the Silver River up to the heaven, in case the Cowherd might chase across the river. Unable to approach the Silver River now, the Cowherd had to go back depressed, hoping to figure out another way.

Back at home, hearing the kids' crying for mom, the Cowherd was heartbroken.

Seeing both the Cowherd and the kids crying sorrowfully,

The Comic Book on the Story of the Cowherd Chasing after the Weaving Maid while Carrying two Bamboo Baskets (Author: Wang Suda)

the bull said, "Cowherd, you've taken care of me for years, and now I am dying. After my death, you could wear my skin and then you can fly to the sky." Finishing those words, the bull closed its eyes and died. The Cowherd did as the bull told, and found himself really able to fly. So he put on the bull's skin, carried on his kids, and continued to chase after the Weaving Maid.

The Cowherd flew up to the sky, shuttling among the shining stars, and after long time of chasing, the familiar Silver River was finally in his sight. The Weaving Maid seemed to be right on the other side of the river. The Cowherd was very excited and the kids waved to their mother happily, at the same time, the Weaving Maid saw her husband and children coming and waved back instantly.

However, the moment when the Cowherd tried to cross the river something invisible blocked his way. The fact is, the Queen Mother had seen the coming Cowherd and to prevent him she made a virtual stroke with her gold hair pin over the Silver River, then the river became impassable.

From then on, the Cowherd can only gaze across the Silver River at the Weaving Maid, who waved back at him from the other side. They tried to talk with each other, but they can't hear clearly; they tried to write to each other, but nobody can send the letter. Finally they figured out a way: their letters are tied to the cattle whip or the weaving shuttle, then thrown across the river to each other. Today, we can still see one bright star on either side of the Milky Way in autumn nights, representing the Cowherd and the Weaving Maid separated by the Silver River. There are two small stars in the front and the back of the Altair, symbolizing the two kids carried by the

Meeting on the Magpie Bridge on Every Double Seventh Day

Cowherd. A little farther from the Vega, there are four stars in the shape of a rectangle, resembling the weaving shuttle thrown to the Cowherd. And not far from the Altair, there are three stars in the shape of a triangle, looking like the cattle whip thrown away to the Weaving Maid.

In that way, the Cowherd and the Weaving Maid passed on their yearning to each other. The Silver River may separate them, but their true love still get together.

The deep love and perseverance of the couple through years finally made the Heaven Emperor yield a little, who permitted them to meet once on the seventh of the seventh lunar month each year. And touched by their true love, many fairies in heaven volunteered to help the Weaving Maid cross the River on that special day; even the magpies, envoy of good news on love, came to help the couple by making a bridge over the River. As the Cowherd and the Weaving Maid were allowed to meet only once in a year, they can't help shedding tears while expressing each other's longing in the reunion. Thus when it rained in some places on Double Seventh Day, it was said that the Cowherd and the Weaving Maid were shedding tears.

There are different versions of the legend about the Cowherd and the Weaving Maid in different places of China, yet the main plots of which remain similar. First, the Weaving Maid in heaven fell in love with the kind hardworking Cowherd. Then they got married and gave birth to a boy and a girl, leading a happy life with the husband working out in fields and the wife weaving at home. However the Queen Mother in heaven objected their marriage and separated them by drawing out a heaven river with her gold hair pin. Finally, the couple got to meet once a year on Double Seventh Day. These stories all reflect people's longing for beautiful love and free marriage in the ancient agricultural society.

The Legend of Kuixing

According to ancient legends, the birthday of Kuixing was on the seventh day of the seventh lunar month. In fact, Kuixing was the incarnation of the Star of Champion, which is the first star among the constellation Big Dipper and belongs to one of the Twenty-Eight Stars. The Star of Champion, also called the Star of Wisdom, was in charge of the fortune in examinations, therefore many ancient scholars would worship the Star of Champion on Double Seventh Day, praying that their diligent study through years would be worthwhile and the Star of Champion would bless them with good official position. Therefore, if some scholar had won the first place in the imperial examination, he would be said to have "bounded into championship".

In the folklore, Kuixing was born on the seventh of the

seventh lunar month. His childhood was quite miserable, living as an orphan because his parents passed away when he was a baby. Fortunately he was adopted by a kind knowledgeable teacher, who appreciated his diligence and devotion to study, treating him kindly as a family member. The teacher was not rich himself, but he never treated Kuixing shabbily, not only providing him a stable life but also teaching him to read and write. Soon Kuixing laid a solid basis of knowledge under the teacher's guidance. However, Kuixing was considered ugly

Lame Kuixing

with pockmarks on his face and a crippled leg, and he was often bullied by other children for his appearance and orphanage. Every time when he felt sad for others' insult, the teacher would comfort him, encouraging him to turn rage and sorrow into advancing motives. In all, with the company of the teacher, Kuixing grew up happily despite poverty and bully in the life. But, happy times slipped away quickly. When Kuixing was in his teens, the teacher died from a fatal disease. Before his death, the teacher said to Kuixing: "It's a pity I cannot see you become the Number One Scholar in the Imperial examination. After I died, you should be cautious in words and action, diligent in study and stick to your dreams…" The teacher breathed his last without finishing his words.

The decease of the teacher was a huge blow to Kuixing, and sorrow deprived him of appetite for three whole days. Later, persuaded by warm-hearted neighbors, Kuixing summon up his spirits to bury the teacher. In the following three years, Kuixing followed his teacher's advice strictly, devoted to his study whole-heartedly.

Three years later, Kuixing went to attend the county examination and passed it successfully. Then he attended the province examination and achieved satisfying results as well. The neighbors and friends all came to Kuixing's home to congratulate him. After the celebration, Kuixing packed up and said farewell to everyone, ready to go to the capital for the imperial examination. Before leaving, he didn't forget to visit the tomb of his teacher and said goodbye to him in tears. Eventually, his years' diligence did not disappoint him, and he gained the first place in the imperial examination.

Having become the Number One Scholar, Kuixing felt relieved of all hardship and went into sound sleep. In his dream, he saw the magnificent imperial palace, the noble queen, gongs and drums clearing the crowded road for his three-day tour, and his town fellows coming a long way to congratulate him... When he woke up joyful, he thought of his teacher gratefully, so he went to the window, made a kowtow to the moon, and said: "Teacher, your words are well kept in my mind. In the future, I would be cautious in behavior, trying my best to be successful in my career and to benefit the world, which is my way of showing gratitude to you!" The next day did bring the drums welcoming him, and he went to the imperial palace ambitiously, kneeing down, waiting for the honor flower bestowed to him by the queen. But something unfortunate happened at that time. When the queen walked to Kuixing with the honor flower, she suddenly saw the ugly face of Kuixing, and thinking a ghost had come out at daytime, she got shocked into a faint instantly. This aroused the rage of the emperor, who immediately ordered guards to drive Kuixing out of the imperial palace and deprived him of his title of Number One Scholar.

The trick of fate agonized Kuixing greatly. He went back to hometown, feeling ashamed and helpless about his own ugly appearance. When kind-hearted town fellows got the news, they all came to comfort him, "Never mind, Kuixing! The queen must be afflicted with some disease and happened to faint at that time. Though it's unlucky this time, as a rare talented scholar you will win the first place again in the next imperial examination!" The encouragement of town fellows

The Kuixing Pavilion on the top of Chongleigang Mountain in Nanhai District, Foshan City, Guangdong Province

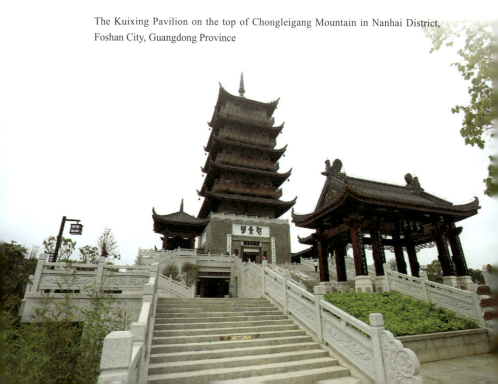

implanted Kuixing with confidence again, and he studied harder for another three years.

The kuixing Pavilion on the top of Choyleigang Mauntain in Nanhai Pistrict,Foshan City,Guangdong Province.

Three years later, the imperial examination was held on time. Kuixing packed up and left home for the capital to attend the examination as before. Once again, he was chosen as the Number Once Scholar; and once again, he frightened the queen to faint and got cast out of the imperial palace. After another miserable three years, hearing that the old emperor had died and the queen of the new emperor was adept with both pen and sword, Kuixing went to attend the examination hopefully again. However, fate would not stop its jokes on Kuixing and the same tragedy happened to him again. This time when Kuixing was cudgeled out the palace by guards, he broke down completely, walking and laughing crazily, keeping yelling "ghost, ghost…" Suddenly, he heard someone sighed: "Too difficult! His Majesty has issued a decree that all scholars chosen out of the imperial examination must possess both talent and good looks. Poor Kuixing! There is no chance for him in this life!" Instantly outrageous, Kuixing shouted to the sky: "Both talent and good looks? Then, Heaven! Why do you let me come to this world?" His roar shocked heaven and earth, causing storming rain with lightning and thunder. Kuixing took off his clothes in sorrowful indignation, stood in the rain naked, then jumped into the huge waves of the East Sea.

The suicide of Kuixing alarmed the Dragon King in the East Sea, who at once ordered the Immortal Turtle to rescue him, hence Kuixing survived fortunately. Finally, the Jade Emperor heard the story of Kuixing. Moved by his miserable experience and great talent, the Jade Emperor bestowed him the honor of Number One Scholar and the right of managing scholars and examinations.

As Kuixing can control scholars' luck in examination, many scholars would worship him solemnly on his birthday – the seventh of the seventh lunar month, which gradually becomes an important custom on Double Seventh Day.

3. Birthland of Double Seventh Culture

Stories on the Cowherd, the Weaving Maid and Double Seventh Day are widespread in China, and it is not unanimously agreed as to the genuine birthplace for Double Seventh Culture. One school holds that the love story between the Cowherd and the Weaving Maid occurred initially in Yiyuan County, Shangdong Province, as there is such a local saying – "As there is the Silver River in heaven, so there is the Yihe River on earth". Another school says the home of the Cowherd and the Weaving Maid was located in Heshun Country, Shanxi Province, which is reflected from the names of two local places: "South Heaven Pool" and "Cowherd Valley Village". A third school thinks that the central birthplace for the legend of the Cowherd and the Weaving Maid should be Lushan County, Henan Porvince, where a lot of succeeding stories on the Cowherd and the Weaving Maid are still spreading. A fourth school insists that the birthplace of the story on Double Seventh Festival is Yunxi County, Hubei Province, because in addition to a local saying – "As there is the Silver River in heaven, so there is the Tianhe River on earth", there is the Cowherd Temple and the Weaving Maid Mountain at the end of the Tianhe River. Last is the school who regards

Nanyang City, Henan Province as the birthplace for Double Seventh Culture, as two villages there are respectively named from the Cowherd and the Weaving Maid, and the bridge between these two villages are regarded as the dating place of the couple.

Yiyuan County, Shandong Province: "As there is the silver River in heaven, so there is the Yihe River on the ground

The legend of the Cowherd and the Weaving Maid was initially recorded in the poem "Large East States" from *The Book of Songs*, which includes such lines as "Three stars make up the Constellation of Weaving Maid" and "Bright is the Star of Cowherd". As studies have proved, the geographical location of "Large East States" mentioned in The Book of Songs spans across Linzi City and Qufu City in Shandong Province. Since Yiyuan County is just located between Linzi and Qufu, it could be considered as the geographic core of "Large East States".

"As there is the Silver River in heaven, so there is the Yihe River on earth" – this is a popular saying spreading in Yiyuan County, Shangdong Province, where the 574-kilometer-long Yihe River starts its flowing. Interestingly, the "Yihe River"

The Cowherd and the Weaving Maid Scenic Area in Yiyuan City, Shandong Province

and the "Silver River" pronounce quite similar in Chinese. Now the only ancient Chinese architecture site concerning the legend of the Cowherd and the Weaving Maid is on the Daxian Mountain, Yanya Village, Yiyuan County, while facing each other across the Yihe River are the Weaving Maid Cave and the Cowherd Temple, built first in the Tang Dynasty. The landscape pattern around the river and its banks corresponds with the constellation pattern "The Altair – the Milky Way – the Vega" in the sky with a striking likeness, forming a spectacle manifesting the mysterious unity of heaven and man. The Cowherd Temple, initially built as a two-storey pavilion, has become a magnificent building now after repeated repairing and rebuilding, possessing three palaces with black bricks, green tiles and painted brackets. In the main palace, there are statues of the Cowherd and his children, accompanied by a golden statue of the bull. And the courtyard is quiet and secluded with ancient cypress trees.

There is a Cowherd Village beside the Cowherd Temple, where most people share the family name "Sun", identical with the family name of the Cowherd – Sun Shouyi. The history of the village can be traced back to the Ming Dynasty. The villagers call themselves descendents of the Cowherd, pass down the story of the Cowherd and the Weaving Maid from generation to generation, and maintain such customs as raising silkworms, weaving cloth and fetching Double Seventh Water, etc.

With an elevation of 532 meters and a forest coverage rate of 96%, Daxian Mountain enjoys a good ecological environment characterized by steep cliffs, huge rocks, and lush pines and cypress. The Yihe River girdling the foot of the

The Niulang Temple in Yiyuan County of Shandong Province

Daxian Mountain is compared to "The Silver River on Earth", the length of which is 3 kilometers, forming a water area larger than 50 km^2.

There are many stone tablets on the Daxian Mountain, most of which are not well-preserved in form, but related somehow to the legend of the Cowherd and the Weaving Maid in content. For example, one stone tablet raised in the 20th year of Jiaqing Period of Qing Dynasty is engraved with two poems entitled "Ascending the Weaving Maid Tower", the author of which is a Qing poet Wang Songting. Third and fourth lines of this poem record clearly and beautifully the story of the Cowherd and the Weaving Maid:

"It seems the Silver River descended down from the heaven,

And the Cowherd and the Weaving Maid were still in this world."

The scenic area of the Cowherd and the Weaving Maid in Yiyuan County is endowed with dense cultural flavor, including not only scenic spots like the Weaving Maid Spring, the Weaving Maid Cave, the Weaving Maid Tower, but also rare plant species like leave-loaded-seed gingko and geological wonders like angular unconformity. The leaf-loaded-seed gingko is a unique tree species in China, rarely seen in the world as the fruits of the tree are loaded directly on its leaves. The local people are rich in imagination, calling a pool of spring there as the tear left by the Queen Mother, and the red cherry as the Love Fruit in a romantic way.

Because of the perfect harmony between nature and culture, Yiyuan County of Shandong Province is entitled as "The Hometown of the Cowherd and the Weaving Maid" and "The Birthplace of Chinese Love Culture". In June, 2008, *The Legend of the Cowherd and the Weaving Maid* in Yiyuan County was included into the second batch of national intangible cultural heritage list.

Heshun County, Shanxi Province: Folk Memories Long Preserving Double Seventh Culture

Heshun County of Jinzhong City is located in the Taihang mountainous area and on the bank of two Zhanghe Rivers, belonging to the east part of Shanxi Province. Due to the laggard development in traffic and economy, Heshun County is rated as a national-level poverty-stricken county. However, in the area less than 10km^2 from the South Heaven Pool to the Cowherd Valley, there are at least 20 scenic spots concerning the story of the Cowherd and the Weaving Maid. The overall environment there is quite similar to what is narrated in the story of the Cowherd and the Weaving Maid, and local villagers pass the story as well as the customs related to Double Seventh Festival from generation to generation.

The district around the South Heaven Pool and the Cowherd Valley belongs to the middle part of Taihang Mountains. The Tianhe Range forms a north-to-south bar, separating South-Heaven-Pool Village from the outside world.

In the area of 10 km² with Tianhe Range as the center, many names of place, such as Cowherd Valley, Magpie Mountain, South Heaven Gate, Tianhe Pool, Old Bull Mouth, etc. corresponds properly with the story of the Cowherd and the Weaving Maid. The district is considered as the birthplace of the Chinese love story with its beautiful scenery, precipitous peaks, mist-covered villages and heavenly atmosphere.

A lot of memories on Double Seventh Culture are long-preserved in South-Heaven-Pool Village of Heshun County. Records of Heshun County written in the period of the Republic of China (1912—1949) reads: "On Double Seventh Day, maids usually sprout five kinds of corn in earthen wares, and pray to the Cowherd and the Weaving Maid for handicraft skills." Many villages would prepare delicious food, set firecrackers, paste window paper-cuts, beat gongs and drums for "Welcoming the Weaving Maid Home". Today, the South-Heaven-Pool Village still keeps the custom of "Watching Sky" on Double Seventh Day. People set tables or sacrificial boards southward in the yard, offering cooked beans with stems and corns wrapped in leaves.

The story told in the South-Heaven-Pool Village is basically the same with folklore from other places, only more vivid and enriched. According to villagers here, the Cowherd ranked as the third child in the family, living in the Cowherd Valley only a few miles away from the South Heaven Pool. His uncle Qin Sihai lived in the South-Heaven-Pool Village, making a living by trading salt, who finally told the Cowherd the bathing place and time of the Weaving Maid and prompted the couple to meet and love each other. Original residents in the village were divided into eight family groups with different family names

Cowherd-and-Weaving-Maid Cultural Festival Held Annually in Heshun County of Shanxi Province

like Li, Qiao, Zhang, He, Lv, Cao, etc., just identical to the family names of "Eight Immortals". When the Queen Mother sent heaven soldiers to capture the Weaving Maid back from earth, the Eight Immortals had ever exerted magic power to resist heaven soldiers and gods. That's why there exist such scenic spots nowadays as Eight Immortal Cave, Nezha Pagoda, Donkey Rolling, and Heaven Marshal Li's Pagoda.

On the night of every Double Seventh Festival, villagers in Heshun County would set tables in the south of the yard, offering cooked beans with stems, corns wrapped in leaves and a kind of steamed bread named "Small Sacrifice". On that day, local villages would prepare delicious food, set firecrackers, paste window paper-cuts (mainly with the designs of the Cowherd and the Weaving Maid), and beat gongs and drums for the celebration. Local people call the ceremony "Welcoming the Fairy" or "Welcoming the Weaving Maid Home".

Owing to innovative measures, heavy investment and steady work, Heshun County has made great progress recent years in excavating, sorting, rescuing relics and publicizing its cultural brand. In 2006, Heshun County was named "Hometown of Chinese Culture on the Cowherd and the Weaving Maid"; and in 2008, "The Legend of the Cowherd and the Weaving Maid" was officially announced by the State Council to enter the second batch of national intangible cultural heritage.

Heshun County has been holding Chinese (Heshun)-Cowherd-and-Weaving-Maid Culture Travelling Festival since 2007, improving its national influence gradually by means of cultural brand and tourism. Wise Heshun people turn the cultural advantage from the legend of the Cowherd and the Weaving Maid into industrial advantage, infusing cultural connotation into tourism, improving overall competitive ability in an economic world by attracting investment and talents to help enlarge market, therefore bringing a new charm to the traditional theme of loyal love.

Lushan County, Henan Province: Hometown of the Cowherd, Famous Place of Love

According to Records of Lushan County, "There is a Cowherd Cave and a Cowherd Temple in the Lufeng Mountain, and anyone praying there for the sick livestock would work wonders." There is a Sunyi Village in Xinji Township, Lushan County, Pingdingshan City, Henan Province, where exists an opinion that the prototype of the Cowherd is Sun Zuyi, the ancestor of the village. The view seems to be supported by historical sites, natural scenery and local customs related to the story of the Cowherd.

Different from the widespread story elsewhere, there is vivid follow-up description to the legend of the Cowherd and the Weaving Maid in Lushan County.

It is said that after being captured back to weave clouds of brocade, the Weaving Maid was very melancholy, missing her husband and children all day long, while the Cowherd and his children was heart-broken as well on the ground. Since their living place was only 2.5 kilometers from the South Heaven Gate on the peak of Lushan Mountain, the children often walked there to ask for the meeting of their mom. The general guarding South Heaven Gate was sympathetic to the family, allowing them to enter privately. Then the Jade Emperor in Heaven became fond of his grandchildren, also permitting them to come freely. Even the Queen Mother was no longer as strict as before in supervising the Weaving Maid, so the relationship between heaven and earth became harmonious gradually. The Cowherd was buried on the south slope of Lushan Mountain after his death, and his descendents in Sunyi Village called themselves "Grandsons of the Cowherd".

Later, the descendents of the Cowherd inherited the estate along the slope of Lushan Mountain. They showed filial piety to ancestors, and appoint a dozen of days each year as festivals to invite the Cowherd and the Weaving Maid back to the village, such as the Eighth of the Twelfth Lunar Month, Spring Festival, the Eighth of the Second Lunar Month, Cole Flower Festival, the Third of the Third Lunar Month, Double Seventh Festival …

The Lufeng Mountain beside the Sunyi Village, the Cowherd Cave on Lufeng Mountain, the Nine Fairies Pool in the west, Auspicious Cloud Taoist Temple on the peak ..., all these scenic spots seem to be telling the moving story of the Cowherd and the Weaving Maid.

The natural environment around Lufeng Mountain is very good, and local people have got used to raising cattle since old times. Different from other places, Sunyi Village in Xinji Township keep the custom of raising but not king cattle in each household, and dead cattle would get buried there. Besides, Lushan County has been famous for silk production since ancient times, and the silk from Lushan County is also called "Weavings of the Weaving Maid" or "Weavings of the Fairy".

Today, Xinji Township is a well-known plantation site of grape, which is also related to the story of the Cowherd and the Weaving Maid. According to the legend, when the Cowherd and the Weaving Maid met on Double Seventh Day each year, girls on the earth could hear the couple whispering if they were under grape trellis. And there is the custom of Skill-Praying on Double Seventh Festival in Lushan County, namely, praying to the Weaving Maid for handicraft skills and for a good marriage.

In Xinji Township, a large-scale fair is held on Double Seventh Day annually. It is testified that Double Seventh Festival fair has a history for at least several centuries, consisting of activities like singing traditional opera, beating gongs and drums, and setting off firecrackers, for the so-called purpose of "Welcoming the Fairy" or "Welcoming the Cowherd and the Weaving Maid Home".

For nearly a thousand years, people in Lushan County have firmly believed that the story of the Cowherd and the Weaving Maid did occur in reality. There is a folk song about the Cowherd and the Weaving Maid long popular in locality, which shows reminiscence and admiration for the love story, retaining dense cultural flavor. It goes like this:

"There is a Lushan Slope on earth,

Connected with the Silver River in heaven.

When the Cowherd and the Weaving Maid meet,

The world is overflowing with happiness."

In 2009, Lushan County was entitled as "Hometown of Chinese the-Cowherd-and-the-Weaving-Maid Culture". From then on, Lushan County has held a series of folk activities for Double Seventh Festival annually, aiming to further exploit the rich cultural resources on the legend of the Cowherd and the Weaving Maid, to deepen the cultural influence of folk customs, and to display the cultural glamour of Lushan County.

Yunxi County, Hubei Province: As there is the Silver River (i.e. Milky Way) in heaven, so there is the Heaven River (i.e. Tianhe River) on earth.

There is a poem of the Qing poet Wang Shude, describing the touching scene in the ancient story of the Cowherd and the Weaving Maid. It reads:

"Thousand of mountains and valleys are singing the praise

Of the profound love of the Cowherd by the Tianhe River.

Clothes wet by splashing waves, the couple were meeting on the bridge,

Which would turn into magpies returning to forest in a short moment."

The "Tianhe River" mentioned in the poem is also regarded as the birthland of Double Seventh Festival, or of love between the Cowherd and the Weaving Maid.

"As there is the Silver River (i.e. Milky Way) in heaven,

so there is the Heaven River (i.e. Tianhe River) on earth" –
this is a popular saying among the people of Yunxi County,
Hubei Province. The Tianhe River is the third biggest river
in Yunxi County, Hubei Province, originating from Shanxi
Province with a total length of 69 km, and 63 km of which
flows through Yunxi County. To the west of the Tianhe River,
there are three rivers, respectively the Maiyu River (pronouncing
similar to "Beauty River" in Chinese), the Xianhe River (literally,
Fairy River) and the Guixian River (literally, Returning Fairy
River); while to the northeast of the Tianhe River, there is a
Yangjia River. The names of the rivers indicate the fairy on
one side and the mortal human on the other side, just like the
fairy in heaven and the Cowherd on earth separated by the
Silver River, telling an everlasting love story. The close relations
between Yunxi County and the ancient legend showed through
the faithful love between beautiful women and sincere men in
locality.

Yunxi County of Hubei Province is quite competitive in
claiming to be the birthplace of the culture on the Cowherd
and the Weaving Maid. It is said that the a note from the
Japanese poem collection Manyoshu has pointed out, that the
love story of the Cowherd and the Weaving Maid just occurred
beside the Tianhe River in Yunxi County, Shiyan City, Hubei
Province. The source of the name for the Tianhe River in
Yunxi County cannot be traced back, yet it is certain that the
name has existed and never been changed since ancient times.
The Chinese character "xi" in the name of the county "Yunxi"
suggests direction of the place, and Yunxi County should be the
place corresponding to the fairy story about the Altair and the
Vega. The Tianhe River in Yunxi has not only the same name as

the river in the fairy story, but also a correspondent geological layout with the position of stars in sky, which prompts the forming of special customs in locality.

On the mountain north to the Tianhe River mouth, there still remain the relics of the Cowherd Temple, where the story of the Cowherd and the Weaving Maid is still spreading. This mountain is called the Goddess Mountain, because it is said to be the place where the Queen Mother of the West cultivated herself to be a goddess, and where she held Peach Banquets to treat all different immortals. Nowadays you could still find a lot of scenic spots on the top of the mountain, including Goddess Temple, Ancient Tree Witnessing Descending of Fairies, Stone Boat of Eight Immortals, Peach Garden, Spirit Palace, Stone Forest, Dragon Head Incense, etc. On the banks of upstream Tianhe River, there are two mountains gazing across at each other, called the Cowherd Mountain and the Weaving Maid

The Night Scene of the Tianhe River in Yunxi County

Mountain by local people. On the mountain near midstream Tianhe River in Shimen Bay, Tianfeng Village, Chengguan Township, there is a stone figure about ten feet high, called "Stone Grandma" as it looks like a women; While there is another stone figure on the Hugai Mountain to the north side of the county, called "Stone Grandpa" as it resembles an old man. These two figures are said to be the incarnations of the Cowherd and the Weaving Maid. According to the legend, when the Cowherd carrying a pair of children was just going to catch up with the Weaving Maid, the Queen Mother drew a Heaven River to divide them up. Then the Cowherd and the Weaving Maid had no other way but gazing at each other far away, and with time passing, they finally turned into mountains on two sides of the Heaven River. The beautiful scenery of the Tianhe River was written into some classical poems in Yunxi County, for example:

"Cloud reflections and shimmering waves are glad to be sleepless

In this cold river where Starlight from the sky shines down.

Low and soft song of lotus picking is heard midnight

Out of some travelling boat with music of flute."

This poem describes how nice the Tianhe River looks like, when it reflects millions of stars on the night of Double Seventh Festival.

The Tianhe River in Yunxi County of Hubei Province has a name reminding us of touching legendary stories, has the water fostering fine ecological surrounding and kind people, and has a geological appearance and a cultural history leaving room for its descendents to inherit and create beauty. All relics, records and folk heritages are powerful evidence that Yunxi county of Hubei Province echoes loudly the legend of the Cowherd and the Weaving Maid, therefore it is honored as the birthplace of the love story on Double Seventh Festival.

Nanyang City, Henan Province: Birthplace of the Love Story between the Cowherd and the Weaving Maid

Beside the national road about 10km west of Nanyang City, Henan Province, there stands a large sign – "Niujia Village". That is a plain village with a small population of 300 plus people, but it has gained a reputation for being regarded as the birthplace of the love story between the Cowherd and the Weaving Maid.

From the legend, it can be roughly concluded that Double Seventh Festival should originate in the Han River area of the Chu State in history, as the love story between the Cowherd and the Weaving Maid had got wide-spread by the Han Dynasty. The document concerned reads, "The real name of the Cowherd is Ruyi, a native of Sanglin Village in Nanyang City. After the Weaving Maid descended to the world and got married to the Cowherd, she taught women in Nanyang to raise silkworms, draw silk from cocoons and weave it into brocades." The folk story popular in locality also says, about 10km west of Nanyang City there is a Niujia Village famous for producing good cattle since ancient times, and more peculiarly, there is a Cowherd living in the village. What's more, there remain a lot of relics concerning the legend and the customs about Double Seventh Festival in the Han River area.

According to the memory of local old people, beside Niujia Village there used to be a bridge, with a stone tablet standing by the side. The face of the stone tablet was engraved with a Altair, below which was a bull, and a man was raising a whip standing in front of the bull. On the left corner there was a Vega, inside which a woman with high topknot hairstyle was sitting on her knees. Between the two stars there is a Heaven

The Magpie Bridge in the Donghu Park of Wuhan City

River. This stone tablet is now stored in the Han Cultural Museum of Nanyang City in Henan Province. While no more than 2 km to Niujia Village there is a Shiwa Village, called also as "Weaving Maid Village" by local people. For around a thousand years, there has existed a local tradition that girls from Shiwa Village do not marry into Niujia Village. The reason is, people in Shiwa Village still hold that if their girls marry boys in Niujia Village, they couldn't accompany each other long in marriages, though they may love each other, just like what happened to the Cowherd and the Weaving Maid. Local people also see the Shiliu River between these two villages as the Heaven River created by the Queen Mother.

In addition to the places mentioned above, there are other places said to be the birthplace of the story of the Cowherd and the Weaving Maid, such as Xingping City of Shaanxi Province, Xiangyang City of Hubei Province, Changbai Mountain area, ect. And there are even media reports that "different places are grabbing for the honor of being the birthplace of Double Seventh Festival". Opinions on this topic may not agree to each other, but all arguments comes to one conclusion that all Chinese people cherish the traditional culture greatly, and the popularity of the story on Double Seventh Festival manifests people's continual pursuing for beautiful love.

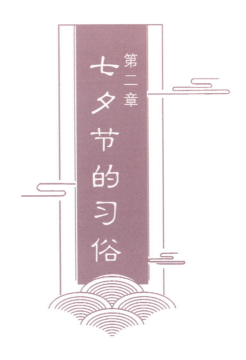

第二章 七夕节的习俗

七夕节在我国古代很盛行，上至达官贵人，下至平民百姓，都热衷于过这个古老而又浪漫的节日。然而，清代以后，七夕与其他一些传统节日一样，逐渐被人们淡忘。

2006年5月20日，七夕节被列入第一批国家级非物质文化遗产名录。许多民俗学者与商家也极力复兴七夕，七夕重新回到人们的视野当中。七夕等传统节日的复兴意义深远，尤其对于年轻人来说意义重大——使他们更深入地了解中国的传统文化，更好地继承中华民族传统美德，增强民族自豪感。现在，七夕节已普遍被认为是中国的"情人节"，其在年轻人中的影响力已经超过从西方传入的2月14日"情人节"。

一、
中国古代的七夕习俗

七夕节源于汉代。唐宋诗词中，妇女乞巧被屡屡提及，唐朝和凝有诗说"阑珊星斗缀珠光，七夕宫嫔乞巧忙"。《开元天宝遗事》记载：每逢七夕，唐玄宗便与妃子在清宫夜宴，宫女们受皇帝影响各自乞巧。这一习俗在民间经久不衰，代代延续。

宋元时期，七夕乞巧相当隆重，京城中还设有专卖乞巧物品的市场，世人称之为"乞巧市"。人们从七月初一就开始置办乞巧物品，乞巧市上车水马龙、人流如潮，到了临近七夕的时日乞巧市更是车马难行，观其风情，似乎不亚于最盛大的节日——春节，说明乞巧节是古人最为喜欢的节日之一。

后来，牛郎织女的爱情故事被融入乞巧节，民间姑娘信以为真。于是每到农历七月初七，在牛郎织女"鹊桥会"时，姑娘们就会来到月下，抬头仰望星空，寻找银河两边的牛郎星和织女星，希望能看到他们一年一度的相会，乞求上天让自己能像织女那样心灵手巧，祈祷自己也能有个称心如意的美满婚姻，久而久之便形成了七夕节。

（一）东汉时期

七夕节乞巧的风俗，最晚应该在东汉时期形成。东汉崔寔《四民月令》里写道："七月七日……设酒脯、时果，散香粉于筵上，祈请于河鼓、织女，言此二星神当会，守夜者咸怀私愿。"另外，东晋葛洪的《西京杂记》中也有关于七夕的记载，"汉彩女常以七月七日穿七孔针于开襟楼，人俱习之"，这是古代文献中关于七夕祈愿乞巧的最早记载。可以看出，这一始于汉代的节日活动的内容主要是向双星乞愿和穿针乞巧。

○上海一家机构组织的汉代乞巧表演

（二）魏晋南北朝时期

魏晋南北朝时期出现了大量描写七夕的诗歌。这个时期，七夕节的活动已经很兴盛，活动内容丰富多彩。根据文献记载，主要有以下几种：

1. 七夕穿针

《萧纲诗选》中的一首诗中写道："怜从帐里出，想见夜窗开。针敧疑月暗,缕散恨风来。"这首诗写得很有意思,说的是七夕晚上穿针,由于光线不够明亮,老是穿不上针。主人公想必是位姑娘,从床帐里跑出来,打开房间的窗户,可是她还是穿不上针,只得责怪月光暗,微风把她的线绳吹散了。

○ 穿针乞巧

2. 喜珠应巧

南朝梁宗懔《荆楚岁时记》里说:"是夕,陈瓜果于庭中乞巧。有喜子网于瓜上以为符应。"说的是于七月七日夜晚在院子里摆好各种瓜果,如果有蜘蛛爬上去结网就说明乞巧的愿望得以应验。为什么有织女把"巧"托付给蜘蛛? 一般的解释是,蜘蛛吐出来的丝很细很软,很像人织出来的线。古时候人们织布首先是要把棉花捻成细线,然后在织布机上织成布。蜘蛛如此灵巧地吐丝,织出的网很有规则,与织布机有异曲同工之妙。

3. 晒书晒衣

七夕前后正是暑热转凉的季节,古人习惯将家中的藏书、衣服拿出来晾晒一番。晒书、晒衣的风俗在魏晋时期很流行,《世说新语》

里面记载了一个有意思的故事。有一个人叫郝隆，是个行为放达不羁的人。在七月七日这天，他看到很多人都把家里的书拿出来晒，认为大家这是在炫富、炫藏书，很是看不惯。于是他就把自己的上衣脱光，然后跑到太阳底下去晒。别人见他这样感觉很奇怪，于是都问他这是在做什么，他回答说"我在晒书"。别人都是把书本拿出来晾晒或者炫耀，却没有像他这样把自己满腹的才学知识拿出来晒的，可见这人也是有些才学，所以才敢如此。

（三）隋唐时期

隋唐时期，七夕风俗基本沿袭了旧时传统，但其内容更为丰富。穿针乞巧的针孔已发展到五孔、七孔、九孔等，并且以蛛丝卜巧的习俗很兴盛。

据《长恨歌传》记载，每到七夕之夜，唐玄宗与杨贵妃都会在华清池游览设宴。那时宫女们便会在庭院中陈列各种瓜果，向牛郎星、织女星祈求恩福，而且还会捉蜘蛛放到盒子里，等到第二天早晨起来观看蜘蛛在盒子里织网的情况，如果蛛网很密那么此人获得的巧就多，蛛网稀少则暗示获得的巧少。"民间亦效之"，可见当时这种活动最初是在宫廷和上流社会兴起，随后才传到民间百姓家里的。

隋唐时，民间还有七夕节"祈子"的说法，宫府作坊的织工也要在七月七日这天祭拜机杼。唐宋诗词中，妇女乞巧被屡屡提及，唐代以七夕为题或以七夕引发感叹的诗歌作品大致有 68 首，50 位诗人以此为题填词作赋，由此可见七夕节在唐代受重视的程度。

唐、五代时，北方民间多以七月六日为"七夕"，宋太宗曾颁布诏令恢复古制，至今仍有在七月六日过七夕节的。

（四）宋元时期

宋元时期，七夕乞巧相当隆重，活动也是丰富多样。宋元时期商品经济十分发达繁荣，京城中设有专卖乞巧物品的市场，世人称之为"乞巧市"。《醉翁谈录》记载："七夕，潘楼前买卖乞巧物。自七月一日，车马嗔咽，至七夕前三日，车马不通行，相次壅遏，不复得出，至夜方散。"在七月一日就出现了交通拥挤的场面，七夕节的前三日车马已经挤得不能动弹了。从人们购买乞巧物的热情上可以推测出当时乞巧节在人们心目中的地位。

宋代民间的七夕庆祝活动也是五花八门，别具特色。元代还出现了新的七夕活动，比如悬挂鹊桥图、穿鹊桥衣的习俗。

○投针验巧

（五）明清时期

明代七夕节的习俗更为多样。《宛暑杂记》记载，"燕都女子，七月七日以碗水暴日下，各自投小针，浮之水面，徐视水底日影，或散如花，动如云，细如线，粗如椎，因以卜女乞巧"。说的是北京一带的女子在七月七日这一天，放一碗水在太阳底下，然后各自向碗里投小针，当针浮于水面时，观看针在水底的日影，以出现的各种日影形状判断得巧与否。在南方广州一带，则承袭古代七夕曝衣书的风俗，还出现了取圣水的习俗。《广州府志》载："七月七日，曝衣书，家汲井花水赐之，以备酒浆，曰圣水。"广西部分地区也有取水的习惯。

清代前期的七夕节，在福建、广东、浙江等地又演变成七娘会。七娘会的参加者都是未婚的姑娘，她们自己筹资，用通草、色纸、芝麻、米粒等制成各种式样的花果、仕女、器物、宫室等，并且在七夕前日这天把针线、脂粉、古董、珍玩、花生、时果等多种东西列在庭内八仙桌上，供大家评赏。等到初七这天开始迎仙、拜仙、拜牛郎等，活动仪式很复杂。清代后期，在山东一带又演变出七月七日贺牛生日的习俗。有人认为这是因为牛在牛郎、织女的故事里发挥了巨大作用的缘故，还有人认为牛是一种埋头苦干的勤劳动物，为人类的农业生产作出了很大的贡献，所以要纪念一下这个大功臣。在江浙一带的民间，还有用槿柳叶洗头发的习俗，据说在此日洗发，可以让自己的头发变得像织女的头发一样乌黑发亮、美丽动人。

〇广州天河区东圃珠村摆七娘活动中的贡案

二、
七夕的趣味乞巧活动

　　到了现代，七夕节活动依然丰富多彩。很多老一辈人依然坚守传统节日习俗，穿针乞巧，摆瓜果于庭院应巧，拜织女娘娘；一些年轻恋人则接受了西方文化的影响，通常在七夕这天会送给自己的爱人一份"情人节"礼物，或者一起去看电影，用多种方式来度过属于他们自己的节日。

　　在传统节日习俗方面，首推"七夕乞巧"活动。七夕节又被称为"乞巧节"，因为织女是个心灵手巧的天仙，所以在这天晚上，年轻的姑娘和少妇都要向织女"乞巧"，希望自己也能拥有一颗聪慧的心、一双灵巧的手。于是，七夕便被赋予了"爱情美满"和"心灵手巧"这两种涵义，围绕这两个主题形成了丰富多彩的民俗活动。

　　"乞手巧，乞貌巧，乞心通，乞颜容，乞我爹娘千百岁，乞我姊妹千万年。"七夕节最普遍的习俗，就是女性在七月初七的夜晚进行的各种乞巧活动，主要有"穿针乞巧"、"投针乞巧"、"喜珠应巧"、"兰夜斗巧"四种形式，此外还衍生出其他一些方式。乞巧的方式大多是姑娘们穿针引线验巧，做些小物品赛巧，摆上些瓜果乞巧。

　　各个地区的乞巧方式不尽相同，各有趣味。有的地方乞巧活动

○明人仿仇英《汉宫乞巧图》（局部）

很简单，只是陈列瓜果乞巧，如有喜蛛结网于瓜果之上，就意味着乞得巧了。还有的地方吃"巧巧饭"：七个要好的姑娘集粮集菜包饺子，把铜钱、木针和红枣分别包到三个水饺里，乞巧活动以后，她们聚在一起吃水饺，传说吃到钱的有福，吃到针的手巧，吃到枣的则能早日成婚。

（一）穿针乞巧

这种节日习俗始于汉代，盛行于南朝，是最早的乞巧方式。穿针分为两种：一种是七夕当晚，姑娘们聚在月光下面，借着月光穿针引线，哪位姑娘可以穿过去，便是得巧了。另一种是在七夕那天的中午，姑娘们将针投在水面上，观察针在水中的影子，来看自己是否得巧，这被称为浮针或投针。

　　最早的穿针、浮针以及投针都是在月下进行，乞巧活动都在七夕当晚举行。随着习俗的不断发展，当中有些习俗发展为在七夕中午进行，以观测太阳投射的影子。早先的月下穿针，是伴随着穿五孔针、七孔针、九孔针的传说，乞巧活动将女红才艺与游戏化的竞赛结合在一起，充满了竞技的意味，在比赛过程中得到巧，也有实至名归之感。后代的浮针、投针，则更似占卜，是否得巧更多取决于运气，这使得许多小姑娘都产生了患得患失的感觉。

（二）喜蛛应巧

　　这也是较早的一种乞巧方式，其俗稍晚于穿针乞巧，大致起于南北朝。蜘蛛与七夕乞巧关系颇深。究其原因，大致有三点：一是秋初，蜘蛛正活跃，要它织网，一般不会令姑娘们失望。二是蜘蛛织网，织女织布，同是巧手。女子们看不到织女织的布，那么就看看蛛网，希望能得到某种启示、某种灵感，或感受到蜘蛛织网的灵妙之气，使

○蜘蛛织网有喜兆

自己的织布之技有所提高。三是古有"蜘蛛集而百事喜"之说，民俗中有蜘蛛预兆喜事的说法，乞巧时用蜘蛛，可增加喜庆气氛。

用蜘蛛验乞巧结果，也有诸多不同。一种是检验瓜果上有无蜘蛛网。七夕之夜，陈瓜果于庭中以乞巧，次日，如果瓜果上有蜘蛛网，就是乞得巧了，否则就是没有乞到巧。有的地方，女子将瓜削成花瓣状，放在盘中，再在瓜上放一针，然后，在庭院中举盘望拜河汉，默企织女赐巧，然后将瓜盘放在庭院中的桌子上。过了一会儿，去看上面有无蜘蛛网，以验是否乞到巧。

另一种是看蜘蛛网的疏密。七夕之夜，姑娘们捉蜘蛛，放在一个小盒子里。第二天，开盒观察，以蜘蛛网的疏与密，验证得巧的少与多。此习俗自唐朝开始，历代有之。宋代文献记载，是要检验所结蜘蛛网是否圆整，将蜘蛛放在小盒子里，次日验看盒内蜘蛛网是否圆整。蛛网若圆整说明乞到了巧，不圆整则说明没有乞到巧。

还有的地方，是男孩子在七夕之夜将蜘蛛放在一个盒内，第二天来验看蜘蛛网，以此来乞文，也就是乞求擅写文章的技巧。这个习俗是由女子将蜘蛛放在盒里验丝乞巧演变而来的。

（三）迎仙得巧

广州的乞巧节独具特色。七月初六、初七两个晚上，姑娘们都身穿美丽的衣服，头戴漂亮的首饰，将自己打扮得十分精致，来拜祭神仙。每晚的三更到

○七夕节夜晚，女孩子拜祭神仙

五更，都要拜祭七次。拜完神仙以后，姑娘们便借着灯影穿针，哪

位姑娘能将彩线顺利穿入针孔中，便是得巧了；如果不能，那便是输巧了。

（四）投针验巧

七夕节活动的主要参与者是少女，而节日活动的内容又是以乞巧为主，故而人们称这天为"少女节""女儿节"。这一天，少女都用盆子盛满水，对着太阳，水中漂一根针；然后从这根针在水中的倒影，来测试是否乞巧成功。

这是七夕穿针乞巧风俗的变体，源于穿针，又不同于穿针，是明清两代盛行的七夕节俗。明朝《帝京景物略》说："七月七日之午丢巧针。妇女曝盂水日中，顷之，水膜生面，绣针投之则浮，看水底针影。有成云物花头鸟兽影者，有成鞋及剪刀水茄影者，谓乞得巧；其影粗如锤、细如丝、直如轴蜡，此拙征矣。"《直隶志书》也说，良乡"七月七日，妇女乞巧，投针于水，借日影以验工拙，至夜仍乞巧于织女"。

（五）集会乞巧

姑娘们聚在一起，行乞巧之俗，游玩嬉戏，更有情趣。这种习俗，各地有所不同。

广东"七娘会"。广州旧时过七巧节非常热闹，尤其是清代、民国年间，民间流传着许许多多有趣的风俗。除了节日来临之前精心准备各种奇巧的手工制品，还要专门将谷种和绿豆放入小盒里浸至芽长二寸，用来拜神。广州人多从初六晚开始至初七晚，一连两晚，姑娘们穿上新衣服，戴上花饰，打扮一新，宛若仙女。先是焚香点

○清代陈枚绘《月曼清游图·七月·桐荫乞巧》

烛，对星空跪拜，称其为"迎仙"；然后大家围坐在八仙桌旁，进行各式各样的游戏。有的吟诗作对，行令猜谜；有的穿针祭拜乞巧；有的演唱粤曲，弹琴吹箫等。欢庆至半夜十二点时，人们将所有的灯彩、香烛都点燃，一片辉煌，喜迎七姐，到处人声鼎沸，非常热闹。最后欢宴一番才散去。

胶东"拜七姐神"。胶东地区的人们在七夕那天要拜七姐神。年轻妇女穿上崭新的衣服，汇聚一堂，一起在庭中祭拜七姐神，口中还唱着动听的七夕歌谣："天皇皇，地皇皇，俺请七姐姐下天堂。不图你针，不图你线，光学你七十二样好手段。"不少地方的少女还制作"巧花"，她们用面粉制作牡丹、莲、梅、兰、菊等带花的饼馍食品，即巧果，还有巧菜（巧菜指在酒盅中培育麦芽）。人们正是在七夕这天用巧果、巧菜来祭祀织女，祈求幸福。

嘉兴"七夕香桥会"。 在浙江嘉兴塘汇乡古窦泾村，每年七夕，人们都赶来参与庆祝活动，一起搭建香桥。所谓"香桥"，就是用各种粗长不等的裹头香搭成长四五米、宽约半米的桥梁，并在桥梁上装上栏杆，在栏杆上再扎上五色线制成的花。夜晚，人们便祭祀牛郎、织女双星，祈求幸福，然后再将香桥焚化。这种仪式象征着牛郎、织女已走过香桥，欢天喜地地相会了。由此可见，这香桥是由传说中的鹊桥演化而来的。

○现代大学生的聚会比巧

（六）造型乞巧

七夕，人们造彩棚、彩桥、仙桥、牛郎织女以及众仙等，供乞巧之用，这是节俗与民间工艺的结合。北宋开封，每逢七夕，人们用竹子、木头、麻秸等材料搭小棚子，棚子上糊上彩色绸缎，做成一栋仙楼，并刻上牛郎、织女以及随从的人像，放在楼中，以这种方式乞巧；或只剪纸成仙桥，牛郎、织女相会于桥上，他们的随从各列两边。

（七）种巧菜、做巧花、扎巧姑

山东荣城有两种活动，一种是培育"巧菜"，即少女在酒杯中培育麦芽；另一种是制作"巧花"，即由少女用面粉塑制作各种带花的食品。

陕西黄土高原地区，在七夕节的夜晚也有举行各种乞巧活动的风俗。七夕前妇女们往往要扎穿花衣的草人，谓之"巧姑"，不但要供瓜果，还栽种豆苗、青葱。在七夕之夜各家女子都手端一碗清水，剪豆苗、青葱，放入水中，用看月下投物之影来占卜巧拙之命，还穿针走线，竞争高低。同时，还举行剪窗花比巧手的活动。

三、
七夕的养生习俗

　　"烟霄微月澹长空，银汉秋期万古同。"七月七日是七夕，七夕佳节是中国最具浪漫色彩的传统节日，许多趣味盎然的七夕风俗，深深地浸润了中医药文化。

（一）配方治病防病

　　七夕是适宜配药的日子，很多地方有配药的习俗。人们常用松柏等入药配方，甚至还主张饵松实、服柏子、折荷叶等，这种神奇的药丸以七月七日的露水调配合成，服后可延年益寿。中医认为，松子能健身心，滋润皮肤、延年益寿；柏子香气浓郁，能养心安神、止汗润肠；荷叶能清热解暑、升发清阳、凉血止血。
　　七夕时还常选用一些比较实用的药方治病。如晒槐汁治痔：将槐树枝切成小段，煎煮至药液呈绿色，先熏后洗痔疮处，有清热凉血、清肝泻火的作用，疗效很好；煎苦瓜治眼疾，苦瓜能清暑涤热，可治赤眼疼痛。《生生编》载其"除邪热，解劳乏，清心明目"；摘瓜蒂治下痢，瓜蒂被《本经》列为上品，治疟功效明显。

七夕，闽西客家人习惯用仙人草、冬瓜块和水熬煮，再用洁净的瓦坛密封贮存，以治疗发热、头痛、中暑、惊风。这是有医学根据的，《本草求原》说仙人草能"清暑热，解脏腑结热毒，治酒风"，《本草再新》说冬瓜"除心火，泻脾火，利湿祛风，消肿止渴，解暑化热"。

（二）储水辟邪防病

七夕节储水，是广西、广东一带的特殊习俗。人们认为用"双七水"洗浴，能够消灾除病，强身健体。所谓"双七水"，也就是说，七夕这天鸡鸣之时，人们就争先恐后去河边、溪边取水，取回后要用新瓮盛起来，待傍晚时分，用来给全家老小沐浴。

关于"双七水"的一种传说是这样的：七夕的前一天晚上（即农历七月初六）是牛郎与织女一年一次的相会时间，可是相会时间只有一个晚上，在破晓之前他们必须分开。在分开的时候，织女会伤心地哭泣，她的眼泪落到人间，化成了雨，即为"双七水"。

七夕储水还有一种民间传说：七夕节这天，天上的七仙女们会来到河里洗澡，仙女洗过的水，不仅沾了仙气，而且是不会变质的。广西等地居民都会在这一天灌储"七夕水"和"冬瓜水"，用来沐浴、泡茶、煮饭，甚至用来治疗温热病、中暑、发烧等疾病。

七夕那天，村民们便把米放入"双七水"中浸泡，用以煲饭、煮粥，有助于养生。余下的部分还会存起来，留待小孩出现小病痛时，加上千日红等其他草药一起煮成药茶，给小孩服下，有去火、消肿、除热痱的功效。

据说用"双七水"洗浴能散发出诱人的体香，对异性有奇异的吸引力，会增加爱情运。同时，用"双七水"沐浴，可消除晦气。

七夕还流行用脸盆接露水。传说露水是牛郎织女相会时的眼泪，如抹在眼上和手上，可使人眼明手快，用它给小孩煎药杀虫效果好。中医认为，露水可以入药，煎煮后可制润肺杀虫的药剂，用它将治疗疥癣、虫癞的散剂调成外敷药，可以增强疗效。

○七夕习俗——脸盆接露水

（三）煎汤洗发美颜

妇女七夕洗发，也是特别的习俗，在湖南、江浙一带都有此记载。湖南《攸县志》记载，"七月七日，妇女采柏叶、桃枝，煎汤沐发"。有些地区的未婚女子，喜欢在节日时用皂角树等树的液浆或枝叶汁兑水洗头发，传说这样做不仅可以使青春美丽常驻，而且可以尽快找到如意郎君。这当中除了女性祈愿仙子佑护之外，也有一定的医学道理。用皂角树枝叶煎汤沐发，能够清热化湿、祛除多余脂肪、通畅毛囊，不会刺激头皮，对防脱发和乌发效果颇佳。

这项习俗，大约和七夕"圣水"的信仰有关。人们认为，七夕这天取泉水、河水，就如同取银河水一样，具有洁净的神圣力量。有的地方直接叫它"天孙（即织女）圣水"。因此，女性在这天沐发，也就有了特殊意义，代表用银河里的圣水净发，必可获得织女神的护佑。

在广东惠州，有七夕泡一盆七色花水让女人更美的说法。七色花也就是七种花，必须是没有毒性的花，例如米兰花、玉兰花、香花草、茉莉花、玫瑰花、康乃馨、大红花等。相传在七夕午夜时，七仙女与董永相会，如果看见有人把七色花泡的水盆放在露天的地方，就会施下仙水，让有情人终成眷属。在这个时候泡的花水，女人用来洗脸洗发会更美。

○ 云南汉服志愿者再现古代花草沐发场景

（四）吃"巧食"强身健体

七夕节的饮食风俗，各地不尽相同，一般都称其为吃巧食，其中多为吃饺子、面条、油果子、馄饨等。如吃云面——此面得用露水制成，吃它能获得巧意。许多民间糕点铺喜欢制一些织女人形象的酥糖，俗称"巧人""巧酥"，出售时又称其为"送巧人"，此风俗在一些地区流传至今。

七夕的应节食品，以巧果为最出名。巧果又名"乞巧果子"，款式极多，主要成分是小麦面、油和糖蜜。宋朝时，市街上已有七夕巧果出售。若购买一斤巧果，其中还会有一对身披战甲，如门神的人偶，号称"果食将军"。巧果的做法是：先将白糖放在热锅中翻炒，把它熔为糖浆，然后和入面粉、芝麻，拌匀后摊在案上用擀面杖擀

091

薄，晾凉后用刀切为长方块，然
后折成梭形面巧胚，入油炸至金
黄即成。手巧的女子，还会捏塑
出各种与七夕传说有关的花样。
此外，乞巧时用的瓜果也可做多
种变化，多是将瓜果雕成奇花异
鸟，或在瓜皮表面浮雕图案，称
其为"花瓜"。

七夕夜"拜织女"是少女、
少妇们的大事。祭拜供品包括茶、
酒、新鲜水果等，"五子"（桂圆、

○包装精美的七巧果

红枣、榛子、花生、瓜子）更是少不了。焚香礼拜默默祷告后，这
些供品就成了女子宵夜的食物。五子的药用价值很高：桂圆有开胃益
气、养血健脾、补心安神、补虚长智之功效；红枣味甘、性温，能补
中益气、养血生津；榛子有"坚果之王"的美称，主益气力；花生滋
养补益，有助于延年益寿；瓜子具有清肺化痰、润肠通便等功效。

四、七夕节的其他习俗

（一）拜织女

　　"拜织女"是少女、少妇们的事。她们大都是预先和自己朋友或邻里们约好五六人，多至十来人，联合举办。举行的仪式，是于月光下摆一张桌子，桌子上置茶、酒、水果、"五子"（桂圆、红枣、榛子、花生、瓜子）等祭品；又有鲜花几朵，束红纸，插瓶子里，花前置一个小香炉。那天，约好参加拜织女的少妇、少女们，斋戒一天，沐浴停当，准时都到主办的家里，于案前焚香礼拜后，大家围坐在桌前，一面吃花生、瓜子，一面朝着织女星座默念自己的心事，如少女们希望长得漂亮或嫁个如意郎君、少妇们希望早生贵子等，都可以向织女星默祷。一群年轻姐妹往往玩到半夜才散去。

（二）拜魁星

　　俗传七月七日是魁星的生日。魁星掌文事，想求取功名的读书人特别崇敬魁星，所以一定在七夕这天祭拜，祈求他保佑自己考运亨通。魁星，为北斗七星的第一颗星，也称"魁首"。古代士子中状元时称"大魁天下士"或"一举夺魁"，都是因为魁星主掌考运的缘故。

根据民间传说，魁星爷长相奇丑，脸上长满斑点，又是个跛脚。有人便写了一首打油诗来取笑他："不扬何用饰铅华，纵使铅华也莫遮。娶得麻姑成两美，比来蜂室果无差。须眉以下鸿留爪，口鼻之旁雁踏沙。莫是檐前贪午睡，风吹额上落梅花。相君玉趾最离奇，一步高来一步低。款款行时身欲舞，飘飘度处乎如口。只缘世路皆倾险，累得芳踪尽侧奇。莫笑腰枝常半折，临时摇曳亦多姿。"

然而，这位魁星志气奇高，发愤用功，竟然高中了。皇帝殿试时，问他为何脸上全是斑点，他答道："麻面满天星"；问他的脚为何跛了，他答道："独脚跳龙门"。皇帝很满意，就录取了他。

另一种完全不同的传说，说魁星生前虽然满腹学问，可惜每考必败，便悲愤得投河自杀了。岂料竟被鳖鱼救起，升天成了魁星。因为魁星能左右文人的考运，所以每逢七月七日他的生日，读书人都要郑重地祭拜他。

（三）拜"七娘妈"

七夕节是"七娘妈"的诞辰日。闽南和台湾民间十分盛行崇拜七娘妈这一被奉为保护孩子平安和健康的偶像。

每年这天，人们三五成群到七娘妈庙供奉花果、脂粉、牲礼等。台湾民众认为，小孩在未满16岁之前，都是由天上的仙鸟——鸟母照顾长大的。鸟母则是由七娘妈所托，因此，"七娘妈"就成了未成年孩子的保护神。婴儿出生满周岁后，虔诚的母亲或祖母就会抱着孩子，带上丰盛的祭品，另加鸡冠花与千日红，到寺庙祭拜，祈愿七娘妈保护孩子平安长大，并用古钱或锁牌串上红包绒线，系在孩子颈上，一直戴到 16 岁，才在七夕节那天拿下锁牌，并到寺庙答谢"七娘妈"多年的保佑。

（四）供奉"磨喝乐"

磨喝乐是旧时民间七夕节的儿童玩物，即小泥偶，其形象多为传荷叶半臂衣裙，手持荷叶。北宋时期，每年七月七日，在开封的"潘楼街东宋门外瓦子、州西梁门外瓦子、北门外、南朱雀门外街及马行街内，皆卖磨喝乐，乃小塑土偶耳"。其实宋朝稍晚以后的磨喝乐，已不再是粗朴的小土偶了，做得越来越精致。磨喝乐的大小、姿态不一，最大的高至三尺，有的以象牙雕镂，有的以龙延佛手香雕成。磨喝乐的装扮，更是极尽精巧之能事，有以彩绘木雕为栏座，或用红砂碧笼当罩子，手中所持的玩具多以金玉宝石来装饰，一对磨喝乐的造价往往高达数千钱。

○ "磨喝乐"小泥偶

（五）为牛庆生

七夕之日儿童采摘野花挂在牛角上，又叫" 贺牛生日"。因为传说西王母用天河把牛郎织女分开后，老牛为了让牛郎能够跨越天河见到织女，让牛郎把它的皮剥下来，披着它的牛皮去见织女。人们为了纪念老牛的牺牲精神，便有了"为牛庆生"的习俗。

（六）晒书晒衣

据《晋书》记载，司马懿当年因位高权重，颇受曹操的猜忌。曹操有意请司马懿出山为仕。有鉴于当时政治的黑暗，汉朝风雨飘摇，司马懿为求自保，便装疯病躲在家里。曹操仍然不放心，就派了一个亲信令史暗中探查真相。时值七月七日，装疯的司马懿在家中晒书，突遇暴雨，司马懿急忙爬起，亲自搬书。令史回去禀报曹操，曹操立即下令要司马懿回朝任职，否则即刻收押。司马懿只好乖乖地遵命回朝。

另有一种人在乱世中以放浪形骸来表达郁闷，他们蔑视礼法，反对时俗。刘义庆的《世说新语》中记载了一则故事。七月七日人人晒书，只有郝隆跑到太阳底下去躺着，人家问他为什么，他回答："我晒书。"这一方面是蔑视晒书的习俗，另一方面也是夸耀自己腹中的才学。

汉代晒衣的风俗在魏晋时为豪门富室制造了夸耀财富的机会。名列"竹林七贤"的阮咸就瞧不起这种作风。七月七日，当他的邻居晒衣时，只见架上全是绫罗绸缎，光彩夺目。而阮咸不慌不忙地用竹竿挑起一件破旧的衣服，有人问他在干什么，他说："未能免俗，聊复尔耳！"由这几则小故事，就可以想见当时七夕晒书、晒衣的风俗有多盛了。

（七）染指甲

染指甲是流传在中国西南一带的七夕习俗。年轻姑娘喜欢先用树的液浆兑水洗头发、沐浴，然后把先前准备好的花草在织女娘娘面前供奉，供奉完将这些花草捣碎，取花草的汁液来染十指。传说这不仅可以使得女子美丽，更重要的是对求婚女子来说，还可以保佑她们找到如意郎君。也有人说七夕染指甲与生育信仰有着密切的关系。

种种趣味盎然的七夕习俗，为我国的民间节日增添了丰富多样的色彩，体现了人们追求身体健康和幸福生活的朴素情感。时至今日，七夕仍是一个富有浪漫色彩的传统节日，但不少习俗活动已弱化或消失，与此同时也派生出一些有新时代特征的七夕活动，如相亲大会、大龄青年联谊会等。

Chapter Two
Customs on Double Seventh Festival

Double Seventh Day was very popular in ancient China, and people of different social positions all loved to celebrate the old and romantic festival. However, after the Qing Dynasty, people gradually forgot to celebrate Double Seventh Day as well as other traditional festivals. Then on May 20, 2006, Double Seventh Festival was included firstly into national intangible cultural heritage list. Many folk culture scholars are trying their best to revitalize Double Seventh Festival, and the importance of the festival is brought back to people. To rejuvenate traditional festivals like Double Seventh Day has a far-reaching significance for Chinese, especially for young people, enabling them to learn more about traditional culture, to inherit national virtues better and to increase national dignity and pride. Now, Double Seventh Festival is commonly considered as Chinese Valentine's Day, producing a larger impact on young people than the Valentine's Day of western countries on February 14.

1. Ancient Chinese Customs on Double Seventh Festival

Double Seventh Festival originated in the Han Dynasty. And in the Tang and Song dynasties, poems often described how women would "pray for skill" on that festival. For example, the Tang poet Wangjian wrote such lines as "Light of stars join the sparkling of pearls on earth; Palace maids are busy in Skill Praying on this night." It was recorded in "Forgotten Tales of the Kaiyuan and Tianbao Periods" that whenever it is Double Seventh Day, Emperor Taizong of Tang would enjoy night banquet with his concubines, and palace maids would engage in the skill-praying activities. This custom was popular among people and got passed down from generation to generation.

In Song and Yuan dynasties, skill-praying activities were quite ceremonious, even "Skill Praying Markets" were set up to sell special objects for the occasion. Dialogues of Drunken Old Men, a book edited by Song Luoye and Jin Yingzhi, says that "On Double Seventh Festival, objects useful for Skill Praying are sold before the Panlou Tower. Since the first of the Seventh lunar month, there have been a lot of horses and carriages. And around three days before Double Seventh Day, the market would be so crowded that horses and carriages couldn't move until midnight." From this paragraph describing the hustling Skill Praying Market, we could know how lively and boisterous the skill-praying activities used to be. People began to buy things for Skill Praying since the first of the Seventh lunar month, and the market was so crowded, the traffic was so heavy when it was near Double Seventh Day, that the merry atmosphere was no less than that of the biggest festival in China – Spring Festival. It shows how ancient people loved this

Skill Praying Day!

Later, the story of the Cowherd and the Weaving Maid was melted into Skill Praying Day, and many folk girls believed in the story genuinely. Therefore on the seventh of the seventh lunar month when the Cowherd and the Weaving Maid were said to reunite, girls would come in front of flowers under the moon, looking up for the two stars on two sides of the Heaven River (i.e. Milky Way), hoping to see their reunion once in a year, praying to be as skillful in handicraft as the Weaving Maid, and praying for an ideal marriage as well. Long time passing, these activities were gradually integrated into customs of Double Seventh Festival.

The East Han Dynasty (A.D.25 – 220)

The custom of Skill Praying on Double Seventh Day should have appeared at latest in East Han Dynasty. In his Monthly Instructions to Four Trades, the East Han minister Cu Shi wrote, "On Double Seventh Day … people set out wine and fruits on sacrificial tables, spreading incense powder on the offerings, praying to the Star of Cowherd and the Star of Weaving Maid for personal wishes, believing the two stars would meet at night." Besides, Ge Hong, the famous Taoist scholar in the East Jin Dynasty recorded in the book Miscellany of the Western Capital, "Palace maids in the Han Dynasty often threaded seven-eye needles on the Kaijin Tower on Double Seventh Day, then common people learned to follow the trend." This is the earliest description on skill-praying activities of Double Seventh Day in classical literature. It may be found that main activities of Skill Praying originating in the Han Dynasty were airing books and clothes in the sun, praying to the double stars and threading needles.

Threading needles for Skill Praying Originating in the Han Dynasty

The Wei, Jin, North and South Dynasties (A.D.220 – 589)

When it came to the period of Wei, Jin, North and South Dynasties, there appeared a large amount of poems on Double Seventh Day. Activities of this festival had developed into popular and various forms, which mainly included the following according to historical literatures:

(ⅰ) Threading Needles on Double Seventh Day

There is an interesting poem about needle threading activities on this festival, which reads,

"How lovely she is coming out of tent!

Opening the night window to see clearer.

She doubts it is the dark moonlight or

The naught wind that make it hard to thread."

In the poem, the girl came out of her tent to open the window, expecting to see clearer the eye of the needle, but still she couldn't succeed in threading the needle. So she blamed that the moonlight was not bright enough, and the wind frequently blew her thread away.

(ii) Watching Spider Web for Skill Divining

Liang Zonglin from the South Dynasty wrote in his Notes about Time in Jingchu Area, "That night, people lay out fruits in courtyard for Skill Praying. If there comes a spider spinning web on the fruits, it is the sign that Skill Praying works." This means the wish of praying skills will be realized if a spider spins web on the fruits laid out in courtyard on the night of Double Seventh Festival. Why the Weaving Maid would give the "skill" to spiders? The general explanation is the silk produced by spiders is very thin and soft, just like the thread spun by weavers. In ancient times, people would first twist the cotton into thin thread before weaving cloth. It is really amazing that spiders could produce thin silk and spin regular webs in such a flexible way.

(iii) The Custom of Airing Books and Clothes in the Sun

In times around Double Seventh Day summer heat would fade away gradually, and ancient people usually moved books and clothes out, drying them in the sun. The custom of airing books and clothes in the sun was quite popular in Wei and Jin Dynasties, which could be reflected from a story recorded in A New Account of World Tales. There was once a man named Hao Long, acting freely without worrying about rules and views of society. On Double Seventh Day, seeing many people take out books into sunshine, he felt contemptuous about the showing-off behavior, so he went to lie topless in the sun. When others asked him what he was doing in puzzlement, he just answered "I am airing my books." As others only aired or showed off their storage of books, he showed his scholarship and knowledge to people. He dared to behave in such a bold way just because he was a man of real talent.

The Sui and Tang Dynasties (A.D.581– 907)

In the Sui and Tang Dynasties, the customs on Double Seventh Day basically inherited old tradition, only with richer varieties of celebration. The number of eye on needles for this occasion had increased into 5, 7, or 9, etc. And it is prevalent to divine the result of Skill Praying by observing spider spinning.

As is recorded, on the night of Double Seventh Festival each year, Emperor Xuanzong of Tang and his consort Yang Yuhuan would make a tour and set banquet in Huaqing Palace; while palace maids would set out different fruits in the courtyard, praying to the Star of Cowherd and the Star of Weaving Maid for bliss. Palace maids would also catch spiders and put them in boxes, and the next morning they would get divination on the effect of Skill Praying from the web in the box. If the web was closely knitted, it meant the girl would be blessed with many skills in handicraft; otherwise she could not acquire enough skills. It is probably that this kind of activity originated first in palace and upper class community, then was imitated by common people and became popular in folk.

In the Sui and Tang Dynasties, there was also the folk custom of "praying to get a child" on Double Seventh Festival, while weavers in official workshop would worship the loom on this day. Later in the Tang and Song dynasties, Skill Praying activities of women were frequently described in poems. There were about 68 Tang poems from 50 or so poets, with Double Seventh Festival in titles or in contents, which shows the importance that people attached to Double Seventh Festival in the Tang Dynasty.

During the period of Five Dynasties of Tang, northerners

in China usually celebrated the festival on the sixth of the seventh lunar month. Emperor Taizong of Song once issued imperial edict to recover the original date for celebration, but not very successfully. Today, some people still celebrate Double Seventh Festival on the previous day.

The Song and Yuan Dynasties (A.D.960 – 1368)

In the Song and Yuan Dynasties, skill-praying activities on Double Seventh Day were very ceremonious and colorful. As commodity economies in the Song and Yuan Dynasties were rather prosperous, there were special markets selling things for the occasion of Skill Praying, called "Skill Praying Market". As is recorded in literature, "On Double Seventh Festival, objects useful for Skill Praying are sold before the Panlou Tower. Since the first of the Seventh lunar month, there have been a lot of horses and carriages. And around three days before Double Seventh Day, the market would be so crowded that horses and carriages couldn't move until midnight." The traffic began to be heavy since the first of the Seventh lunar month, and around three days before there would be a serious traffic jam. The importance of Skill Praying Day for people could be judged from their enthusiasm on buying things for the occasion.

There was a variety of folk celebrations on Double Seventh Day in Song and Yuan Dynasties. For example, there appeared new celebrating activities in Yuan Dynasty, including hanging pictures of the Magpie Bridge, wearing clothes with designs of the Magpie Bridge.

The Ming and Qing Dynasties (A.D.1368 – 1911)

When it came to the Ming Dynasty, customs on Double Seventh Festival became more colorful. It is recorded in Notes Taken in the Public Office of Wanpin County that "On

Double Seventh Day, girls from the capital usually put a bowl of water under the sunshine. Then they throw a small needle onto the water, making it float. The shadows of the needle under the water, in different possible shapes like flower, cloud, thin thread or thick spine, etc., would be observed as the divination on the result of Skill Praying." In other words, on this day girls from Beijing would throw a needle onto a bowl of water under the sun, and watch the shadow of the floating needle, with the aim of divining the result of Skill Praying from the shape of shadow. In the area nearby Guangzhou City in south China, people keep the customs of fetching holy water and airing clothes and books in sunshine. Government Records of Guangzhou City said, "On Double Seventh Day, people usually air clothes and books in sunshine. They also draw water out of the well early in the morning, calling it Holy Water and using it for brewing." Parts of Guangxi Province also follow the custom of fetching Holy Water.

Early in the Qing Dynasty, Double Seventh Festival took the form of "Seven Girls' Meeting" in Fujian, Guangdong and Zhejiang provinces. The attendees of "Seven Girls' Meeting" were all maidens, who at their own cost made artificial flowers, fruits, lady dolls, objects, palaces from materials like rushes, colorful papers, sesames and rice grains, and displayed those things together with their needlework, cosmetics, antiques, peanuts, fruits, etc. on the table in courtyard. On Double Seventh Day, they would take on a series of activities like Welcoming Immortals, Praying to Immortals, Praying to the Cowherd, and so on. Later in the Qing Dynasty, in the area nearby Shandong Province there came into being the custom of Celebrating Bull's Birthday on Double Seventh Day. Some people thought that the bull played a key role in the story of the Cowherd and the Weaving Maid; others hold that the bull deserved people's memory as it contributed a lot to human agriculture by working diligently. In locality along Jiangsu and Zhejiang provinces, people follow the tradition of washing hair by using water boiled with willow leaves on Double Seventh Day, the function of which is said to make one's hair as black and smooth as that of the Weaving Maid.

2. Interesting Skill Praying Activities on Double Seventh Day

Nowadays, people still celebrate Double Seventh Day in various ways. Old generations stick to the traditional customs, like threading needles for the purpose of Skill Praying, setting out fruits in the courtyard, and worshipping the Weaving Maid; while young lovers are influenced by the western culture in a sense, would usually send gifts to their lovers, go to the cinemas or celebrate their festival in other novel ways.

Praying to Immortals on Double Seventh Day

As to the traditional customs for the festival, Skill Praying is one of the most important celebrating activities. Double Seventh Festival is also called "Skill Praying Festival", because the Weaving Maid is regarded so clever and skillful that many young women would pray to the Weaving Maid for skill on this day, hoping to owe intelligence and skill as she does. Hence Double Seventh Festival is endowed with two themes – "beautiful love" and "wonderful skill", around which colorful folk activities were held.

"Pray for my skillful hands! Pray for my beautiful face! Pray for my clever mind! Pray for my parents' longevity! And pray for my sisters' health!" A most popular custom on Double Seventh Festival is the Skill Praying on that night, taking on various forms such as "Threading Needle for Skill Praying", "Throwing Needle onto Water for Skill Divining", "Watching Spider Web for Skill Divining", "Seeking Hided handicrafts as Skill Competition", and so on. Most common ways of Skill Praying for girls are threading needles to test skill, displaying their own handicrafts to compete in skill, and setting out fruits to pray for skill.

Different places are featured with different interesting ways of Skill Praying. Some places hold simple skill-praying activities, for example, by setting fruits out on the table and waiting for spiders to spin webs. Some other places have the custom of having "Skill Meal": Seven girls would make dumplings together, and put a copper coin, a needle and a date respectively into any three dumplings. After Skill Praying, they would eat dumplings together, and the one eating the dumpling with a coin would be blessed with fortune, the one eating the dumpling with a needle would be gifted with skill, and the one eating the dumpling with a date would walk into marriage soon (as "date" and "soon" have the same pronunciation in Chinese).

Threading Needle for Skill Praying

This custom is the earliest form of Skill Praying, originating in the Han Dynasty and booming in the South Dynasty. There were two ways of using needles: firstly, on the night of Double Seventh Festival, girls met under the moon, and anyone who could thread the needle successfully in moonlight was considered as being endowed with skill; secondly, at noon of that day, girls threw needles onto the surface of the water, observing the shadows of the needles to see if they could get the skill, and this activity was called "Throwing Needle" or "Floating Needle".

Earliest activities of threading, floating or throwing needles were carried out in moonlight, and Skill Praying was held on the night of Double Seventh Festival. With the development of customs, some activities began to be held at noon to watch the shadow against the sun. Earliest activity of threading needles brought along stories of threading five-eye, seven-eye or even nine-eye needles. Activities of Skill Praying integrated skills in needlework to competitive games, so it is quite convincing that anyone winning the game would be blessed with skill. While later activities like floating needles or throwing needles were more similar to divination, and whether one will acquire the skill depended more on luck, making many girls anxious about the divining result.

Watching Spider Web for Skill Divining

This is also an early form of Skill Praying, originating around the South and North Dynasties, a little later than the activity of Threading Needle. The spider has a lot to do with Double Seventh Day, the reasons are as follows: First, spiders are usually active in spinning webs in early autumn, seldom letting girls down. Second, spiders spin webs as skillful as the Weaving maid weaving cloth; since girls cannot see the Weaving Maid working, they could watch spiders spinning instead, so as to get some enlightenment and inspiration from

Threading Needle in Moonlight

spiders to improve their own weaving skills. Third, since ancient times there has been a saying – "If spiders spin webs, everything will be smooth." Seen as an auspicious omen in folk culture, the spider is often used to add joyous atmosphere in Skill Praying.

There are different ways to divine the result of Skill Praying by watching spiders. First, people would check if there are spider webs on the fruits or not. On the night of Double Seventh Festival, fruits would be set out in the courtyard, and if they are covered by spider web the following day, it means skill has been bestowed to the owner, otherwise it hasn't. In some places, girl would cut melon into the shape of flower, put it on the plate, and a needle on the melon. She would hold the plate to pray to the Heaven River (i.e. Milky Way), wishing the Weaving Maid would bestow skills upon her, and then leave the fruit plate on the table in the courtyard. After a while, she would go checking if there are spider webs on the fruit plate, to divine the result of Skill Praying.

Second, people would check if the spider web is closely knitted or not. On the night of Double Seventh Festival, girls would catch spiders and put them into boxes. The following day, they would know the amount of skill granted to them by observing the density of spider web in the box. Beginning from the Tang Dynasty, this custom handed down different ages. The literature in the Song Dynasty recorded that a key point was to check whether the spider web is round and regular. Put the spider in a small box, and the next day people would check the shape of the spider web: if it was round and regular, Skill Praying was effective, otherwise it was not.

In other places, boys also put spiders into boxes on the night of Double Seventh Festival, and they watch the spider web the next morning for the purpose of praying for writing skill. This custom is a variety transformed from girls' activity of Watching Spider Web for Skill Divining.

Welcoming Immortals to Get Skill

Skill Praying Day in Guangzhou City is very unique. On Double Seventh Day, girls would make or knit small objects by using colorful papers, threads, rushes or other materials. They also put corns and mung beans in small boxes filled with water, which would be offered as offerings to god when sprouts of around two inches come out of the water, and the activity is called "Praying with Immortal Crop" or "Praying with Holy Vegetable". On the sixth and seventh night of the seventh lunar month, girls would dress themselves up with beautiful clothes and jewels to pray to immortals, and they would worship for three times each night from the third watch to the fifth watch (i.e. from 11:00 pm to 5:00 am). After worshipping, they would thread needles by lamps, and anyone successfully inserts colorful thread into the eye of needle would be granted with skill, otherwise she wouldn't.

Throwing Needle onto Water for Skill Divining

As the participants of activities related to Double Seventh Festival are mainly girls, and Skill Praying is one most important custom on that day, people name the day also as "Girls' Festival" or "Maids' Festival". On that day, many girls put a basin with water in the sun and float a needle on the water; then they observe the shadow of the needle in the water, trying to divine the result of Skill Praying.

That custom is a variety transformed from Threading

Throwing Needle onto Water for Skill Divining

111

Needle for Skill Praying on Double Seventh Day, mainly prevalent in the Ming and Qing Dynasties. Briefs on Scenes and Customs in the Capital of the Ming Dynasty reads, "Women throw Skill Needles onto water on Double Seventh Day. They first put a pot of water in the sun, after a while, there will be a mask on the surface of water, which could float a needle thrown in. Watch the shadow of needle in water, and if the shadow looks like clouds, flowers, birds, beasts, shoes, scissors, wild tomato roots, etc., the Skill Praying is successful. But if the shadow is thick as a hammer, thin as silk, straight as a candle, it is an awkward omen." It was also recorded in Annals of Zhili Province that in Liangxiang Township, "on Double Seventh Day, women would carry out activities of Skill Praying, such as throwing a needle onto water and watching its shadow under the sun to divine the result of Skill Praying, or praying to the Weaving Maid for skill at midnight."

The Custom of Throwing Needle onto Water for Skill Divining Kept Till Today

Getting Together for Skill Praying

Girls getting together to play games is an interesting way of following the custom of Skill Praying, and the custom varies to places.

"Seven Girls' Meeting" of Guangdong Province: It used to be quite joyful and boisterous in Guangzhou to celebrate Double Seventh Day, and especially during the Qing Dynasty and the Republic of China, a lot of interesting customs were popular in folk. In addition to preparing various novel objects before the arrival of the festival, people also put corns and mung beans in small boxes with water, which would be offerings to God when sprouts of two inches or so come out of the water. From the sixth to seventh night of the seventh lunar month, girls would dress themselves up with new clothes, flowers and jewels, as beautiful as fairies. Then they would light incense and candles, and prey to the starry sky, which was called the ceremony of "Welcoming Immortals". Next, people usually sat around the table to have various games: some making poems and couplets, some playing drinking games to guess riddles, some threading needles for Skill Praying, some singing Cantonese operas, and others playing musical instruments. When it was 12 o'clock at midnight, people would light up all lanterns and candles to welcome the arrival of the Weaving Maid. Everywhere was joyous and boisterous, and the celebration lasted deep into night until people finished their banquet and melted away gradually.

In Jiaodong district, there is the custom of "Praying to the Weaving Maid". On Double Seventh Day, young women from Jiaodong district would put on new clothes and meet in the courtyard, praying to the Weaving Maid while singing a beautiful ballad for the occasion: "Holy heaven and earth! We sincerely invite the Weaving Maid from sky! We do not intend to acquire her needle or thread, but learn her great skill in needlecraft!" Girls in many places would make "Skill Flowers" or "Skill Snacks", actually some pies with the design of flowers (of peony, lotus, plum or orchid) on the surface, and they would make "Skill Vegetables" as well, which were usually wheat sprouts in wine cups. They served "Skill Snacks" and "Skill Vegetables" to worship the Weaving Maid and prayed for happiness on Double Seventh Day.

In Jiaxing City of Zhejiang Province there is a traditional activity called "Incense Bridge Meeting on Double Seventh Day". In Gudoujing Village of Tanghui Township, Jiaxing City, people celebrate Double Seventh Festival by making "Incense Bridge" annually. The so-called "Incense Bridge" is a 4-or-5-meter-long and half-a-meter-wide bridge, made from various

The Contest of Threading Needle for Skill Praying on the night of Double Seventh Festival

The cowherd and the Weaving Maid Met on the Magpie Bridge

kinds of incense wrapped in paper, with railings decorated with flowers of colorful threads. At night, people would pray to the Star of Cowherd and the Star of Weaving Maids for happiness, then burn the incense bridge, which represents that the Cowherd and the Weaving Maid have walked over the incense bridge and met in joy. It can be judged that this custom comes from the legend on the Magpie Bridge.

Making Building and Figure Models for Skill Praying

On Double Seventh Festival, some people make models of sheds, bridges, houses, the Cowherd, the Weaving Maid and other immortals for the occasion of Skill Praying, which is a combination of folk custom and handicraft. In the North Song Dynasty, for Skill Praying on Double Seventh Day, people made sheds of bamboo, wood or stalk, decorated them into immortals' towers with colorful silk fabrics, and put figures of the Cowherd, the Weaving Maid and other attendants in the towers. They sometimes cut paper into an immortals' bridge,

115

and put the figures of the Cowherd and the Weaving Maid on the bridge, with attendants following on both sides.

Planting "Skill Vegetables", Making "Skill Flowers" and "Skilled Girls"

In Rongcheng City of Shandong Province, there are two kinds of activity celebrating Double Seventh Festival: one is planting "Skill Vegetables", i.e. girls cultivate wheat sprouts in wine cups; the other is making "Skill Flowers", namely, girls make snacks with designs of flowers.

In loess plateau area of Shaanxi Province, there are all kinds of celebrating activities on the night of Double Seventh Festival. Women usually make straw figures in colorful clothes which were named "Skilled Girls"; they also set out fruits as offerings, and plant bean sprouts and scallions. On the night of Double Seventh Festival, girls would hold a bowl of water, cut the bean sprouts or scallions and put them in water to watch their shadows in moonlight, so the result of Skill Praying could be divined. They also compete in needlework and paper cutting, seeing who is most skillful in handicraft.

3. Customs of Health Preserving on Double Seventh Festival

"Through the smoke of incense a crescent moon hangs in the tranquil sky;

The autumn Milky Way looks the same in thousands of years."

Double Seventh Day is a most romantic traditional festival in China, and many interesting customs of that day show the deep influence of Traditional Chinese Medicine.

116

Filling a Prescription to Cure or to Prevent Diseases

Double Seventh Day is considered suitable time to fill a prescription, and people of many places keep this custom. They usually include pine and cypress in the prescription, and other ingredients like pine nut, platycladi seed or lotus leaves are also regarded medicative. The ingredients could be mixed with the dew of Double Seventh Day and made into a kind of magic pill. If you take one of such pill, you could live 10 years longer; and two, 20 years longer. Traditional Chinese Medicine holds that keeping pine nut in diet could benefit body and mind, moisturize skin and length lifespan; platycladi seed has a strong fragrance with the efficacy of keeping mind quiet, stopping extra perspiration and lubricating the intestines; while lotus leave has the function of crelieving internal heat, elevating lucid Yang energy, cooling blood and stopping bleeding.

On Double Seventh Day people also choose other practical prescriptions to cure disease. For example, they make use of the sap of pagoda tree to cure hemorrhoids in the following way – cutting the branch of pagoda tree into shorter pieces, extracting green sap by boiling them, then fumigating and washing the affected part with the sap, which has a good efficacy of cooling blood and clearing liver-heat. Some people cure eye diseases by using bitter gourd, which could clear summer heat and cure red and sore eyes, as mentioned in Notes on Prolonging Life, bitter gourd is able "to clear pathogenic heat, release fatigue, refresh mind and strengthen eyesight". And bitter gourd pedicel could cure dysentery, regarded as an effective remedy for malaria by Herbal Classic.

On Double Seventh Day, the Hakka in the west of Fujian Province usually boil mesora chinensis and white gourd

117

together in water, then seal and store the water in clear earthen jars for the treatment of fever, headache, heat stroke and infantile convulsion. This is based on some medicinal principle, as the book Source Tracing on Herbal Classic writes that mesora chinensis could "clear summer heat, detoxify the heat in viscera and cure alcoholic wind", while Renewal of Herbal Classic says that white gourd could "clear heart and spleen heat, promote diuresis, expel the wind, diminish swelling, and relieve thirst and summer heat".

Storing Water to Exorcise Evil Spirit and Prevent Disease

Storing water on Double Seventh Day is a special custom in Guangdong and Guangxi region, where people think that bathing with "Double Seventh Water" could exorcise evil spirit, cure disease, and strengthen health. The so called "Double Seventh Water" is the water fetched back from rivers or streams in early morning of Double Seventh Day, which then would be stored in new urns for the whole family to bathe in the evening.

There is such a story on the custom of storing Double Seventh Water: The former night before Double Seventh Day (i.e. the sixth of the seventh lunar month) was the time for the Cowherd and the Weaving Maid to meet once in a year, yet it was too short and at daybreak they had to separate from each other again. Therefore, every time when they had to part, the Weaving Maid would cry sadly, whose tears fell down to earth and turned into rain – the source of Double Seventh Water.

Another folk legend about storing water on Double Seventh Day is: The seven fairies usually came to have a bath in the river on this day, leaving the river water never deteriorating. Therefore, residents around Guangxi Province would store "Double Seventh Water" and "White Gourd Water" on this

Storing Water on Double Seventh Day to Exorcise Evil Spirit

day, for the purpose of having bath, making tea, cooking, or even curing heat diseases, heat stroke and fever, etc. In the times when doctors and medicines were in bad need, this probably became the best traditional medicine for common people.

On that day, many villagers soak rice grains in Double Seventh Water to cook rice or porridge, which is said to be healthy. The rest water would be stored, and if the children get some disease later, the water could be cooked together with medicinal herbs into decoction, which has the efficacy of clearing internal heart, diminishing swelling and removing rashes.

It is said that bathing with Double Seventh Water could make one smell nice, adding one's sexy glamour and increasing one's luck in love. Meanwhile, evil spells could be exorcised

119

through the bathing. Old saying goes that on Double Seventh Festival, if girls wash hair with water mixed with the sap of trees, they could not only maintain youth and beauty but also find their dream lover soon.

It is also popular to collect dew with washbasins on Double Seventh Day, as the dew is thought as the tears of the Cowherd and the Weaving Maid in their meeting. If the dew is applied to one's eyes and hands, one could be sharp-eyed and deft-handed; and if it is used to boil medicine, the effect of expelling parasite is very good for kids. Traditional Chinese Medicine holds that dew could be used in prescription, boiling the medicine with the effect of moistening lung and killing virus, or be mixed together with medicinal powders for external application, increasing the efficacy of curing scabies and favus.

Boiling Beautifying Water to Wash Hair and Bathe

Women washing hair on Double Seventh Day is another

Water Sacrifice Festival on Double Seventh Day in Bama County of Guangxi

special custom of the festival, which could be proved in the records of Hunan, Jiangsu and Zhejiang provinces. Records of Youxian County in Hunan Province writes that, "On Double Seventh Day, women usually pick cypress leaves and peach branches, then boil them in water for the purpose of washing hair." Girls in some places often mix the sap or leave-juice of honey locust tree in the water to wash hair, through which they are said able to maintain youth and beauty, and to find their dream lovers very soon. This custom has some medical basis apart from its superstitious elements. For example, boiled water containing the leave-juice of honey locust tree can clear heat

and remove dampness, take away extra fat and unclog hair follicles; it will not stimulate scalp and has a good effect in preventing hair from dropping or turning gray.

This custom is probably related to people's belief in "Holy Water" of Double Seventh Day. It is thought that water fetched from spring or river on this day is as clean and holy as the water from the Silver River, therefore

The Gleditsia Sinensis, a Unique Tree of China, whose Pod-shaped Fruits have medicinal and cleaning functions it is also called "Granddaughter's (i.e. the Weaving Maid's) Holy Water" in some places. Thus it has a special meaning for women to wash hair on this day, that is, anyone washing hair with the Holy Water of the Silver River will be blessed by the Weaving Maid.

In Huizhou City, a saying has it that making a basin of water with seven kinds of flowers would add beauty to women. The flowers must be non-toxic, such as orchid, magnolia, vanilla, jasmine, rose, carnation, safflower, etc. It is said that on the midnight of Double Seventh Festival, the Weaving Maid and the Cowherd will meet each other. If they see a basin of water with seven kinds of flower left in open places, they will exert magic spell in the water, which could prompt a happy marriage for two lovers and add beauty to a woman washing face and hair with it.

Having "Skill Food" to Improve Health

Diet customs on Double Seventh Festival vary in different places, and people usually call the special food on that day as "Skill Food", including jiaozi, noodle, deep-fried dough stick, wonton, etc. For example, there is a kind of noodle made with the dew of that day, said to be able to endow the eater with skill. And there is a longtime custom in some places for folk pastry cook to make crunchy candy in the form of weaving girls, which is called "Skill Person" or "Skill Candy", and the selling of which is called "Sending Skill Person".

Among all the food for Double Seventh Festival, "Skill Snack" is the most popular one. "Skill Snack", also called "Snack for Skill Praying", is various in its form, with flour, oil and honey as its main ingredients. In the Song Dynasty there had been Skill Snack in the market, and if you bought 500 kilograms of it, you could usually find a pair of figures in it, which are "Generals of Snack", wearing armor just like door gods. The recipe of Skill Snack is as follows: first, stir fry the sugar in hot pan until it melts into syrup; then add flour and sesame into it and mix everything completely; now take out the mixed dough and put it on the kneading board, roll it into a large thin piece; later when it is cool, cut it into small rectangles; last, fold the rectangles into the shape of shuttle and fry it crisp. Women with skillful hands can also shape the dough into different objects related to the legend of Double Seventh Day. Besides, the fruits for Skill Praying could be carved into various flowers or birds, and the melon could be engraved with picture on its skin, called "Flower Melon".

Praying to the Weaving Maid is a big event for girls and young wives on the night of Double Seventh Festival. Sacrificial offerings include tea, wine, fresh fruits, and "five dry snacks"

The Special Dish "Meeting on the Magpie Bridge" on Double Seventh Festival

Skill Snacks on Double Seventh Festival

(longan, red dates, hazelnuts, peanuts, and melon seeds), which could serve as night snacks for girls and young wives after their praying activities. "Five dried snacks" are nutritious with medicinal effects: longan can benefit appetite and spleen, enrich blood and vitality, nourish the heart and calm the nerves, restore deficiency and improve brain; red date is sweet in taste and mild in nature, able to invigorate spleen and replenish qi, enrich blood and engender liquid; hazelnut as "King of Nuts" is beneficial to vitality and strength; peanut as "Longevity Nut" in folk is nutritious and healthy; melon seed has the efficacy of clearing lung, eliminating phlegm and relaxing bowel, etc.

4. Other Customs of Double Seventh Festival

Praying to the Weaving Maid

"Praying to the Weaving Maid" is an activity related merely to girls and young wives. They usually make appointments with their friends or neighbors to hold the ceremony together, in a group from five to a dozen persons. To begin with, they set out sacrificial offerings such as tea, wine, fruits, "five dry fruits" (longan, red dates, hazelnuts, peanuts, and melon seeds), etc. on a table under the moonlight. Then they put several flowers and bundles of red paper into a vase on the table, with a small incense burner in front of the vase. Next, girls and young wives, who have already had a bath and fasted for a day, would gather together on time, burning incense and praying before the table. After that, they usually sit around the table, eating peanuts and melon seeds, speaking silently to the Star of Weaving Maid their wishes, such as becoming more beautiful, marrying a good husband, or giving birth to a son soon, etc. They would enjoy themselves until midnight.

Praying to Kuixing (The Star of Champion)

It is said that Double Seventh Day is the birthday of Kuixing. Kuixing is in charge of literacy and examinations, therefore scholars aspiring to success in examination and career worship him greatly, and they will pray to him on Double Seventh Day for good luck in examination. Kuixing was the incarnation of the Star of Champion, the first star among the constellation Big Dipper and belonging to one of the Twenty-Eight Stars. As the Star of Champion was in charge of the fortune in examinations, when an ancient scholar won the first place in the Imperial Examination, he was described as "The champion of Scholars in the world" or "Bounding into Championship".

According to the folk legend, Kuixing looked extremely ugly with pockmarks on his face and a crippled leg. Somebody even wrote doggerel to laugh at his looks:

"He is too ugly to use any cosmetics,

As none of which could hide his bad looks.

A pockmarked girl would become his perfect match,
And his face would surely remind one of a beehive.
His eyes below his brows are like foot-prints left by a goose,
Which then seems to stamp on his face into a mess.
If he occasionally take a nap in the courtyard,
His wide forehead could catch a lot of falling petals.
What's most interesting is his feet,
One lift higher and one lower in steps.
He hobbles along as if he is dancing,
And passes by in most grotesque shape.
Maybe he is so tired walking in the unsmooth world
That he loses the balance in his gait.
Don't laugh at his half bent back,
It can sway pleasingly while he walks."

However, this despised ugly man was ambitious and diligent, and he got the first place in the Imperial Examination. Then in the palace, when the emperor asked him why he got so many pockmarks on his face, he answered: "A pockmarked face suggests that I could get all stars in heaven!" The emperor continued to ask him why he was lame, and he replied: "Having a crippled leg, I could jump over the Dragon Gate easily!" Hearing that, the emperor was very satisfied and admitted him the Champion Scholar.

Another version of the legend on Kuixing says that, Kuixing failed Imperial Examinations repeatedly in spite of his rich knowledge and great effort, so he tried to drown himself in river desperately. However he was saved by a turtle and finally ascended to the heaven, becoming the Star of Champion. Because Kuixing was in control of the fortune in examinations, scholars all worshipped him solemnly every year on his birthday

– Double Seventh Day.

Praying to "the Seventh Fairy Mom"

In Taiwan and south Fujian province, Double Seventh Day is also considered as the birthday of the Seventh Fairy Mom, who gets extensive folk worship for protecting children's safeness and healthy.

Every year on this day, groups of people come to the temple of Seventh Fairy Mom to offer sacrificial flowers, fruits, domestic powder, animals, etc. In Taiwan, people think that children under 16 are all looked after by the immortal bird in heaven – the Mother Bird – at the request of the Seventh Fairy Mom, who is accordingly the goddess protecting nonage children. When a child is one year old, his pious mother or grandmother usually would prepare rich offerings and two kinds of flowers: cockscomb and globe amaranth, and take the baby to the temple for worship, praying that the Seventh Fairy Mom would protect the child's growth. From then on, the child would wear a coin or a talisman tied with red thread around his neck, which could not be taken off until it is the Double Seventh Day of the year when he is 16, and on that day he should go to the temple again to thank the Seventh Fairy Mom for her years' protection.

Worshiping the Clay Idol "Mohele"

"Mohele" is a kind of clay idol favored by children as a toy on Double Seventh Festival, usually in the shape of a child wearing clothes of lotus leave and holding lotus leave in hand. In the Song Dynasty, every year on Double Seventh Day, there were clay idols Mohele sold in many places of Kaifeng City, such as "fun houses outside Dongsong Gate of Panlou Street, fun houses outside Liang Gate west of city, markets outside Northern Gate, outer street of south Zhuque Gate and inner Mahang Street". In late Song Dynasty, Moheles were made more and more delicate with various sizes and postures, the largest of which was 3 feet high, resembled a real child. Moheles were often carved from ivory or ambergris bergamot, designed in various styles, such as surrounded by carved wood railing with colorful paintings, or staying beneath the cover of red or green gauze, or holding gold or jade toys in hand, therefore a pair of Mohele idols could cost as much as several thousand cash.

Celebrating the Birthday of Bull

Children often pick wild flowers to hang on the horns of bull on Double Seventh Day, calling it "Celebrating the Birthday of Bull". As legend has it that when the Queen Mother of the West separated the Cowherd and the Weaving Maid with a Heaven River, the old bull asked the Cowherd to cut off and put on its skin so that he can fly to see the Weaving Maid, people began to develop the custom of "Celebrating the Birthday of Bull" in memory of the devoted spirit of the loyal bull.

Airing Clothes and Books in the Sun

In the stories, there was a kind of people, who expressed their dissatisfaction with troubled times by acting in an unrestrained and alternative way. The chapter 25 of *A New Account of World Tales* by Liu Yiqing recorded such a story of Hao Long, who lay down under the sun instead of airing books like others on Double Seventh Day. When someone asked him what he was doing, he answered: "I am airing books." His behavior showed his contempt on the traditional custom on one hand, and his boasting of knowledge on the other hand –

Airing Books in the Sun

meaning books were all digested by him.

In the Han Dynasty, the custom of airing clothes created a chance for rich families to show off their fortune, which was deeply despised by Ruan Xian, one of the "Seven Sages of the Bamboo Grove". Therefore, while his neighbors were airing expensive clothes of silks and satin on Double Seventh Day, he hung out shabby clothes on a bamboo pole calmly. When asked why, he just answered: "As I can't avoid the influence of customs, I could only follow it awkwardly." These stories tell us how prevalent the customs of airing books and clothes were at that time.

Dyeing Fingernails

The custom of dyeing fingernails is popular in southwest China. Young girls in many areas first wash their hair and bathe with the mixture of tree sap and water, and then worship the Weaving Maid with prepared flowers; at last they usually crush those flowers and take the liquid to dye their fingernails. It is

129

said that the way can not only make a woman more beautiful, but also bless the women to marry a worthy husband. It is also said dyeing fingernails on Double Seventh Day is closely related to people's belief on fertility.

Various interesting customs on Double Seventh Day have enriched the content of the folk festival, showing people's plain pursuit for health and happiness. Today, Double Seventh Day is still a romantic traditional festival, but some old customs have been weakened or replaced by activities of new times, such as blind-date party, social gathering for singles, etc.

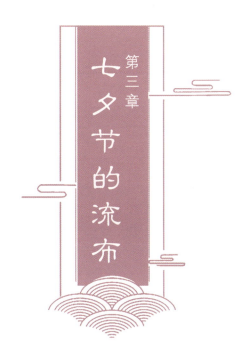

第三章

七夕节的流布

　　七夕节是中国传统节日中最富有浪漫色彩的一个节日，也是中国古人最喜欢的节日之一，尤其是唐宋时期，七夕节盛极一时。但此后，七夕风俗日渐寥落，只是广东、福建等东南地区仍有传承。近代以来，蕴含丰富人文精神和浪漫色彩的七夕节经过人们的改造和挖掘，又重新焕发了生机，显露了其长久的生命力。中国幅员辽阔，地域文化差异较大，但各地的节日活动内容却不尽相同，异彩纷呈。本章撷取北方的山东省、南方的广东省，以及客家人和台湾地区的七夕习俗为代表，以点带面地概括七夕节的流布状况。

一、
山东的七夕节

旧时山东各地都以七夕为节,举行多种多样的乞巧活动。七夕夜晚,抬头仰望天空,便可以看见牛郎、织女在天河相会;在果架下,可以听到牛郎、织女在天上相会时说的脉脉情话。织女心灵手巧,因此每到七夕这一天,少女们就会摆上时令蔬菜、水果,朝天祭拜,乞求织女娘娘赋予她们聪慧的心灵和灵巧的双手,让她们的技艺增进。

山东是七夕文化的重镇,丰富多彩的七巧活动流传于各个地区。

(一)菏泽:包饺子、葡萄架下悄悄话、相思雨

菏泽地区有一种别具一格的"乞巧节"活动,名之"包饺子",这是一种求心灵手巧的风俗活动。在七夕这一天,凡是年轻的未婚女子都可以参与,但必须和七个女子在一起。在七月初七这一天的傍晚,年轻的女子穿上美丽的衣服,然后将采摘的七种不同的花做成饺子馅,包饺子时再放进去七根木针,煮熟以后七个女子一起吃水饺。吃饺子时格外需要技巧和小心,若是咬到针尖,就意味着这

○年轻女子包饺子时往饺子里"藏针"

为最聪明。

民间传说，七夕三更躲在葡萄架下能听到牛郎、织女的悄悄话。在当地老一辈人中流传着这样一个说法，即在七夕的夜晚，在葡萄架下可以听到私语声，若是仰望天空，看到两个大火球碰撞在一起，但凡看到此情景的人眼睛就会瞎掉。因为你触犯了天上的神仙，看到了不该看到的东西，理应受到惩罚。这虽是一种迷信的说法，却颇有趣。

另一种传说：七月七日早晨是见不着喜鹊的，因为喜鹊一大早要赶到遥远的银河为牛郎、织女搭桥，所以这一天的清晨会格外冷清。还有一种传说是七月初七这天必会下雨，那是牛郎、织女的眼泪。牛郎、织女一年方得见一次，相恋的两人相见，自然泪如雨下，人们将七夕下的雨称为"相思雨"或"相思泪"。

（二）曲阜：做巧果巧灯、洗头、晒衣服

曲阜地区流传着在七夕做巧果与巧灯的传统。巧果与巧灯造型五花八门。巧果是少女们用面粉制成荷花、牡丹、菊花、月季、芍药、佛手、玉簪、兰花、海棠、文宫果、玉兰、梅花等造型各异的饼馍食品，巧灯有八仙过海、群仙祝寿、童子拜观音、福禄寿等造型生动的人物灯。相传孔府会将巧果和巧灯作为节日礼品送给各府的本家和亲友。七夕之夜，先从孔府大门，然后沿中仪路到后堂楼各院门口，再到花园各路各景点，皆摆设巧果与巧灯。入夜，府中人坐于庭院中仰望牛郎、织女会面。

曲阜当地人还习惯于七夕之日洗头、晒衣物。女性在这一天都要洗头，据说这天洗头头发会明亮柔软。

○曲阜孔府大门

（三）胶东："偷"青秫秸

胶东地区在乞巧之前有请七姐姐的风俗活动。女子们白天会到田地里去"偷"一些青秫秸，一路上不回头，也不说话，回家后立即扎一神龛，或在土台上搭一小棚，供上织女图。入夜后，女子们再手持秫秸围井台转一圈，请七姐姐位归神龛，然后坐在织女像前，对拍巴掌向织女乞巧。女子们边拍边唱："一巴掌一月一，姐姐教我纳鞋底。二巴掌二月二，姐姐教我绣花裙……"

（四）荣成：做巧菜、巧花

荣成地区庆祝七夕有两种风俗活动：一种名曰"巧菜"，是指女子们在缸中培育麦芽，培育出的麦芽即巧菜；一种名曰"巧花"，是由少女们用面粉塑制的各种带花的食品。

（五）其他各地风俗

山东济南、滨州、淄博等地的乞巧风俗活动相对简单，只陈列瓜果乞巧，若有蜘蛛结网于瓜果之上，就说明乞着巧了。而鄄城、曹县、德州等地吃巧巧饭乞巧的风俗活动颇

○包在水饺中的钱币寓意有福

为有趣：一般七个要好的女子集粮集菜包饺子，并将一枚铜钱、一根木针和一个红枣分别包到三个水饺里。乞巧活动之后，她们相聚在

一起吃水饺，吃到铜钱寓意有福，吃到木针寓意手巧，吃到红枣寓意早婚。

此外，山东各地还流行"穿针乞巧"和"漂针乞巧"。"穿针乞巧"是用芝麻芽或用线穿过缝衣针或特制的七孔针，借着香头的微光，穿针引线，看谁穿上线谁就算是乞得巧了，并且穿得最快者为最巧；"漂针乞巧"是用一碗水在太阳底下晒一中午，然后将针或者谷物的芽放进碗中，让它漂浮在水面，看水底的针影，成各种花纹者为得巧，若针影粗直、细微则是笨拙的征兆。

山东地区乞巧节的节日活动带有比赛性质，类似古代斗巧的风俗。近代的穿针引线、蒸巧馍馍、烙巧果子、生巧芽以及用面塑、剪纸、彩绣等形式做成装饰品等就是斗巧风俗的演变。无棣、长岛等地有做巧芽的习俗。一般在七月初一将谷物浸泡在水中发芽，七夕这天，剪芽做汤。

山东各地乞巧节的饮食一般是面条、水饺、馒头和烙果子等。临沂习惯用储蓄的露水做面条；堂邑将七夕做的面条叫"云面"，意为巧云；昌邑用7种野菜包包子；胶东家家户户烙"巧果子"（先用油、鸡蛋、糖把面粉和好，再用荷花、桃、鱼等模子制成各种花样，最后烙熟），用线穿起来，给小孩挂在脖子上，边玩边吃，亲友之间相互赠送。

二、
广东的七夕节

　　七夕节是我国传统节日中最具浪漫色彩的一个节日，也是过去姑娘们最为重视的日子。相对于北方人七夕吃巧果、吃饺子，岭南地区七夕节的习俗很不一样：拜七姐、七姐诞、七夕取水、染指甲……与其他地方日渐寥落的七习风俗相比，广东的七夕风俗却是一枝独秀、独具一格。直至今日，"七娘会"风俗仍在广东一些地方流传着，

○女红巧物"仙女下凡"

137

如广州珠村的七娘会，就远近闻名，近年来已发展成一个闻名南粤的大规模节会活动。

（一）广东：七娘会

在广东，最重视七夕节的是清代、民国年间。屈大均《广东新语》中记载了清初"七娘会"的盛况。

七娘会活动一般是在少女少妇中进行（男子与老年妇女只能在一旁观看，并行礼祭拜），预先由要好的十数名姐妹组织起来准备"拜七姐"，在六月便要将一些稻谷、麦粒、绿豆等浸在瓷碗里，让它们发芽。临近七夕就更加忙碌，要凑集一些钱，请家里人帮忙，用竹篾、纸扎糊起一座鹊桥并且制作各种各样的精美手工艺品。

到七夕之夜，便在厅堂中摆设八仙桌，系上刺绣台围（桌裙），摆上各种花果制品及女红巧物，大显女儿们的巧艺。有用剪纸红花带围着的谷秧、豆芽盘，盘中点着油灯，灯光透出彩画薄纸灯罩，

○广东望牛墩七夕节展出的"七娘会"工艺品

艳彩夺目；有精心布置的插花，幽香四溢的白兰、茉莉、素馨及其他鲜花插在铜瓷花瓶里；有茶匙般大的荷花、玫瑰、夜合、山茶插在小盆中，一朵真的配一朵假的，真假难辨；有把苹果、桃、柿等水果切削拼叠成各种鸟兽等形状的果盘；有寸许长的绣花衣裙鞋袜及花木屐；有用金银彩线织绣的小罗帐、被单、帘幔、桌裙；有指甲大小的扇子、手帕；有用小木板敷土种豆粟苗配细木砌的亭台楼阁……总之，越细致越显得巧。又用米粒、芝麻、灯草芯、彩纸制成各种形式的塔楼、桌椅、瓶炉、花果、文房四宝及各种花纹和文字的麻豆砌成的供品；还挂一盏盏的玻璃或彩纸的花灯、宫灯及柚皮、蛋壳灯（上雕山水花鸟图案），动物形灯。最惹人爱的，是女儿们用彩绸扎制的精美的雏偶，即布娃娃。雏偶有牛郎、织女及一对小儿女的形象，一般放于上层，下边是吹箫弹琴舞蹈的小儿形象，庆贺双星相会之意。还有"西厢""红楼""杨门女将"等成套的戏剧人物形象；也有瓷塑雏偶，是家长买给小儿女作节日礼物的。另外，少不了陈列化妆用品，如小胭脂盒、镜子、彩梳、绒花、脂粉等，既供织女使用，又供女儿们自用。还有蜡制瓜果、小动物等。此外就是甜、咸点心以及茶、酒、瓜子、花生等食物。必不可少的是烛台、香炉，插上香烛，并用最好的檀香点燃。

女儿们在七夕夜要尽情梳妆打扮，沐浴、洗头发，然后换上锦绸裙袄、旗袍，头上梳发髻，戴上白兰、素馨等花饰；再画眉、抹脂粉、点绛唇、额上印花，用凤仙花汁染指甲。经过这番打扮，女儿们一个个如同仙子下凡，围坐于八仙桌旁，鹊桥边上，进行各种游戏：或自娱自乐，吟诗作对、行令猜谜、穿针祭拜乞巧；或指点天上北斗七星（相传织女是七星姐妹中的一员）及双星，讲述牛女故事、诗文典故；或请来歌姬，演唱粤曲，奏八音乐等，女儿们也自奏琴箫等乐器。这时人们可往各处人家参观乞巧桌陈设，到的人虽多，主人也仍高兴招待。欢庆至半夜十二点钟，为织女下凡之吉时，此时所有的灯彩、香烛都点燃，五光十色，一片辉煌；姑娘们兴高采烈，穿针引线，喜迎七姐，到处欢声鼎沸。最后欢宴一番，这才散去。诚如清代诗人汪仑《羊城七夕竹枝词》听说："绣闼瑶扉取次开，花为屏障玉为台。青溪小女蓝桥妹，有约会宵乞巧来。"

（二）广州：七夕"迎仙"

广州的乞巧节独具特色，除了"七娘会"，"迎仙"这种风俗别具一格。宋人刘克庄曾有诗咏道："瓜果跽拳祝，喉罗朴卖声。粤人重巧夕，灯光到天明。"节日到来之前，姑娘们就预先用彩纸、通草、线绳等编制成各种奇巧的小玩艺儿，还将谷种和绿豆放入小盒里用水浸泡，使之发芽，待芽长到两寸多长时，用来拜神，称为"拜仙禾"和"拜神菜"。

七夕前夜（广州人多从初六晚开始至初七晚，一连两晚），姑娘们穿上新衣服，戴上新首饰，连指甲也涂上了红色，然后把早已准备

○贡桌的茶杯和水果等祭品都是七份

140

好的各式物品，如古董、珍玩、鲜花、水果以及脂粉等摆放在厅堂的八仙台上，还要有一盏油灯放置在"仙禾"或"仙菜"中间。此时，有钱人家的厅堂布置得锦屏绣椅、富丽堂皇，一般人家尽量把厅堂摆设井然。一切都安排停当以后，姑娘们便焚香点烛，对星空跪拜，称为"迎仙"。自三更至五更，要连拜七次。此时，除了邀请亲戚朋友前来做客以外，还要请邻里中相识与不相识的姑娘们一起拜神，观赏巧艺与玩具，高高兴兴，热热闹闹，如巧艺与玩具受到越多人的称赞，主人家姑娘就越高兴，越感到荣耀。广州的姑娘们说，像这样能在众人面前展示手艺，一生是没有多少回的。

拜仙之后，姑娘们手执彩线对着灯影将线穿过针孔（古称"金针度人"），如一口气能穿过七枚针孔者被称为巧手（得巧），穿不到七孔针者则"输巧"。正如唐代诗人所描绘："向月穿针易，临风整线难。不知谁得巧，明旦试看寻。"再后便焚烧纸制的圆盒（梳妆盒），盒里装有纸制的衣服、鞋、脂粉、梳妆镜、梳子等，每样一式七份。祭拜仪式结束后，八仙台上的摆设保持不动，留待翌日（初七）供姑娘们互相串访时参观、评议。到了初七晚，继续如昨晚一样祀神，称为"拜牛郎"，一般由男童主祭。七夕过后，姑娘们所制作的工艺品、玩具等互相赠送，以示友情。

广州七夕拜仙，已婚女子一般不能参加，但新婚后的新娘在过第一个七夕时要举行一次"辞仙"仪式。即在初六晚上祀神时，除了牲醴、红蛋、酸姜等以外，还要加上雪梨或沙梨，表示与姑娘节离别之意。

○拜牛郎

《广州市志》所载，初七日，旧俗还有女子泛舟游石门沉香浦的活动。游艇用素馨花、茉莉花装饰，称为花艇。她们信此日为"仙女淋浴日"。石门浦水质清冽，朝夕日出日落时返照两山，有时会像海市蜃楼一样在天空出现一些景幻。泛舟者若有运气便会看到最奇的出现。故姑娘们七夕游石门沉香浦成为一项重要内容，很是热闹，也成了一个节日习俗。

（三）潮汕：七夕节"出花园"

七夕节这一天，潮汕地区很多满15岁的孩子都要举办一次特殊的仪式——"出花园"，这被称作"特殊的成人礼"。

为什么叫作"出花园"呢？较老的潮汕村民认为15岁以前的孩子，都是在花园里玩耍的。成人以后，就要走出花园，要到外面的世界去经受风雨，去闯世界。在潮汕人看来，"公婆神"的生日是在农历七月初七，也就是七夕。在这一天举行仪式，是表示对"公婆神"的感谢。很多身在外地的孩子，在15岁举办"出花园"成人礼时都要返回老家，举行仪式和宴请亲戚朋友。

七夕一大早，参加"出花园"仪式的孩子要打扮一新，由父母挑着两筐满满当当的祭品，上山去祭拜土地神。祭拜完，就回到村里拜"公婆神"和"十二公婆"。祭拜的房间内墙上还挂着《劝世文》供孩子们观看。临近中午，亲戚朋友们纷纷赶来，热闹的午宴在小村里举行。饭桌上往往有一锅所谓"猪腹内"的菜，包括猪心、猪肝、猪肠等。按照当地人的说法，这叫做"换腹内换肠换肚返大"，也就是盼望孩子成人后快快长大。

在过去的潮汕地区，没到15岁不能算"人丁"，"出花园"之后就跟成人一样待遇了。所以"出花园"这种成人礼在过去很隆重，这种仪式就是给孩子一种暗示，让他们知道自己长大了。在这一天，穿上新衣服、新鞋子，全身上下焕然一新，意味着是在跟过去彻底告别，完全长大成人了。

近来，潮汕地区的"出花园"受现代化冲击，很多程序都大大简化了，比如以前要穿木屐，现在一般就穿普通鞋子。但是，这种仪式还是传承了下来，它已经被列为非物质文化遗产而加以保护。

三、客家人的乞巧节

客家人，是指原籍中原的汉族，历经五次大规模南迁，在南方各省形成的具有独特风貌的客家民系。客家民系是中华汉民族八大民系中重要的一个支系。据估计，全世界约有8000万客家人。客家人在南方地区居住有2000多年历史，主要分布在赣南、闽西、粤东三角地带，梅州、惠州、赣州、汀州被誉为"客家四州"。由于兼融中原文化和南方定居地文化，客家人的七夕节习俗有不少独特之处。

（一）宁化：客家祖地乞巧节

客家祖地福建省宁化县的乞巧节，有鲜为人知的"拜巧"和"食

143

七层糕"的习俗。

　　七月初六，不论男女便开始了"拜巧"的准备工作——制作"巧姐鞋"：一是用各色彩笔在纸上或画或描状元拜塔、鱼跃龙门、文房四宝等吉祥图案；二是在画的下端剪菱花、金钱花等各种剪纸，展示其不凡的聪明才智；三是下面再悬挂一只用红纸剪成的"小鞋子"，男鞋圆头的，女孩则略带尖形。"巧姐鞋"做好后，便被高高地挂在新砍的竹枝上，供人观赏。初七这天，各家结彩棚、绘彩画、写巧书。孩童们兴致特浓，穿戴讲究，要头戴由妇女手工缝制的上面绣有虎嘴、虎须、虎耳朵，形似老虎头的"虎帽"，脚穿模仿古代的"官靴"而制作的官鞋，由父辈亲自带领到文庙孔子神位前拜孔夫子，称为"拜巧"。俗传这一天去拜孔子的孩子会变得更聪明，能念书，长大会做官。拜巧时，敬上香烛，献上供品，跪地叩拜。父辈亦在一旁陪拜，口中念念有词，其大意是，请赐给孩子聪明，保佑能念书之类。也有的孩子要在神位前背诵一段《三字经》或《论语》。

　　入夜，孩童们跪拜于香案前祷告牛郎、织女双星，乞求赐予智

○福建省宁化县客家祖地

慧，然后在大人指导下朗诵"乞求诗"，用毛笔写在红纸上，内容据儿童大小而不同。小的念"七夕庆良宵，双星会鹊桥，儿童勤乞巧，金榜姓名标"。大的则念"今夜为何夜倍明，原来牛女渡天河。家家彩楼重重结，处处诗歌叠叠声。殷勤乞拜三分巧，振起笔尖中头名"。后面续上某年某月某日某某学生沐浴焚香百拜等内容。反复吟诵到月挂中天、时交午夜，也就是牛郎、织女相会之时，才将"乞巧诗"焚于厅前。尔后，家庭主妇端出代表吉祥如意的用米做成的鸡、鸭、鱼、果等，让孩子吃完休息，"拜巧"活动才告结束。这一习俗寄托着客家人勉励后代勤奋读书、早日成才的殷切心愿。另外，宁化还有"引巧""谢巧"和"御巧"的习俗。旧时姑娘长到16岁便算大人了，这一年七夕要举行"引巧"仪式，她必须剪绘7张"巧姐鞋"，图案和剪纸必须各不相同，以示姑娘心灵手巧。到姑娘出嫁的那年七夕，就要举行"谢巧"和"御巧"仪式，她要制作21张花样迥异、图案精美的"巧姐鞋"，以免夫家看不起。

另一独特有趣的习俗是"食七层糕"。这一习俗主要流传于闽西北的治平畲族乡。每年七月初七夜晚，每家都在院内摆上瓜果、茶酒和七层糕，全家围坐一起，边品尝香甜的七层糕，边仰望璀璨的星空，听老人讲述美丽动人的牛郎织女故事。

七夕节做七层糕是闽西北的传统习俗。原来，为了纪念牛郎和织女相会的日子，客家先人们特制这甜香的"七层糕"，敬祀牛郎织女星，久而久之，相沿成俗。每至七夕，乡民们就会自制"七层糕"食用。特别是男女订婚后，每逢七夕日，男家便要送礼给女家，就像春节送年糕、端午节送粽子一样，男家送女家的礼物中便有七层糕。女方收到七层糕后，会切成小块分送给左邻右舍、亲戚朋友，让其品尝，以示求缘吉利。

七层糕与源远流长的七夕文化有着不可忽视的联系。细究七层糕，红糖（红色）象征红红火火，吉吉利利；白糖（白色）象征洁白如玉，纯洁高尚；糕有七层恰与"七夕"数字相符，也就象征七巧节；糯米的黏性与七层糕层层相粘则象征爱情如胶似漆、坚贞不渝。

（二）大田：七月祖宗节

农历七月，俗称"瓜月""巧月""鬼月"。前者的得名，是在时令上适逢瓜果成熟并已上市；而巧月和鬼月，与我国民间自然崇拜与祖先崇拜的传统文化有关。

农历七月十五日为道教的中元节，中元节和清明节、农历十月初一的寒衣节，并称为一年之中的三大"鬼节"，所谓"鬼月"据此产生。

中国人思想淳朴，认为世间万物都是有灵魂的。《礼记·祭法》载："大凡生于天地之间者皆曰命。万物死曰折，人死曰鬼。"从梁代开始，民间就在中元节这日为鬼神庆祝节日。这里所说的"鬼"，一般专指自家已过世的先人。大家通过各种特殊的祭拜方式来缅怀祖先、弘扬孝道，发扬中华民族的优良传统。

在福建省大田县，七月七日过"祖宗节"，七月十五为"补节"。从初一开始，全县各地村民自发起来修路，凡年满18虚岁以及年龄在50岁以下住在村里的男子，都要自觉带上锄具，给村庄所有的道路劈草、挖沟、垫土、换桥木等，是夜会餐，提前准备接祖宗回家过节。

过节其实是很严肃和讲孝顺的。阴阳学认为从午时到亥时属阴，为神鬼等"暗"的东西活动的时间。故此过了中午，各家各户才能带上备好的猪、羊、鸡、鸭及各式米果、果品等，到祖祠由长者主持统一祭拜，然后回到家里再备一份上供。祖祠的祭拜一般要举行读祭文等仪式。

山川的回民过节最早，修路的第二天就开始了，然后七月十五再做“补节”。这一带的人其实都做补节，主节是初七，后者为未能如期回家过节的祖宗另备着。传说当时因为人口稀少，为了躲避土匪，就和旁边的川石、湖坪等村民一起躲进山里，等土匪走了才回来再做节。

东坂的巫姓既是客家又是畲族，他们的过节推迟到七月十四才开始。原由已经无人知晓，只是祖上规定，每年的十四祭祖要杀肥猪，祭祀后的猪肉人人有份，分发到户，所需的猪都由各房按抽签产生的房头家养供给。与此同时，其他人家也要带上三样食品上供，但是也不准相同，一定也得按上年抓阄指定好的带到祠堂里，他们祭祖的供品非常丰富。

由于历史原因，大田明代置县时是从周边的德化、漳平、永安、尤溪等地划入的，因此在习俗和语言上较难沟通，历来就有“隔河不同语，十里不同俗”的特点，且按地域又划分了前路、后路、上府、下府，语言也有前路话、后路话、闽南话、桃源话、客家话之分，但这些同时也构成了大田生动和奇特的文化现象。

跟尤溪渊源较深的后路广平、建设一带，过节也在农历七月十四。后路人的祖宗节的确是“女儿节”，女儿节在大田的意思并不是给女儿做的节日，而是出嫁后女儿们要回娘家孝敬健在父母的节日。后路盛产鸭子，逢年过节家家户户的餐桌上都离不开一盘熏鸭或者腊鸭。于是在节前女儿们都要给父母送米粉和鸭干，就像其他地方端午节女孩子要给父母送粽子和猪腿一样，丝毫马虎不得。当然，除屏山、济阳这些原来靠闽南的地方年节不送礼外，广平人和建设人端午也送礼。

在唐朝开成元年（836年）之前就已经定居在前路魁城的陈姓后人，祖宗节则选在七月十五日与中元节同时做。他们不知从何时起

147

就规定了上供不摆年糕、糍粑等黏性的食物，坚持敬祖宗和鬼神只能上些干的东西。据说如果做了带汤汁的食品祭祖不仅表现为不敬，而且摆过的东西撤下来后会变味而不敢食用。

新中国成立后第一版《大田县志》记载，农历七月初七或十五，各家各户都要备办米粿、三牲祭奠祖先，俗称"鬼节"；还有"七月半，插香线"。七月十五夜，人们把燃香从家门口地上直插到路口。小孩擎着插满燃香的柚子和稻草龙在村道上玩，俗称"柚子灯""稻草龙"；城关下桥张氏放水灯……人们以此祈求田禾大熟、人丁平安、六畜兴旺。

七月过祖宗节虽然在时间上不大一致，但是在大田却被看得相当重要。究其原因，除了传统的孝道思想和道教文化影响外，还有一层关系即跟地里的瓜果成熟有关。大田人六月不做喜事，除生日之类无法回避的以外，据说主要原因是这时正处在青黄不接的时节，六月也因此被戏称为"无米月"。七月则不仅瓜果成熟，而且在春天养下的鸡鸭也刚好长成，加上秋天来临，百草由荣向衰，这时离单季稻的收割和番薯的收起又有一段空闲，整理好道路、吃好点、养足了体力为秋收作准备。如此说来，"瓜月"也好、"鬼月"也罢，两者结合在一起是有一定道理的。

（三）仙游：白糖炒黄豆花生

仙游地处福建沿海中部，湄洲湾南北岸结合部，是莆田市下辖的一个县。

在仙游，这天每家每户都会去做炒豆，材料是白糖、黄豆，还有生花生。黄豆要提前一天浸泡，第二天在锅里炒半熟盛起来备用，花生也是要在锅里炒热后盛起，接着把白糖倒进锅里煮，等糖化了，再把黄豆和花生倒进锅里一起煮。这个习俗已经流传很久了。

（四）梅州：巧结稻草

梅州地处闽、粤、赣三省交界处，也是客家人的重要聚居区。客家人保留的传统习俗，大都是唐宋时期由中原地区的移民带来的，历经千年，已与居住地的风俗融合。

据《梅州客家风俗》记载，梅州客家妇女有"乞巧穿针"习俗；在与岭南稻作文化融合后，演变为"巧结稻草"的习俗。十根长的稻草，由一妇女拦腰抓住中间，另一妇女在两头分别打结，每两根稻草头打结在一起；一头打五个结，另一头打四个结，最后把十根稻草打开，看能否连成一根草绳。若能连成，则得巧，意味着以后遇事巧成。

四、台湾地区的七夕节

台湾和大陆文化同根，骨肉相连，台湾同胞的先辈很多是古代福建的移民，两地的七夕习俗大同小异，共同的节俗活动使两岸人民的距离更近了。在台湾，七夕节又叫"情侣节""女儿节"，是"时年八节"中最富浪漫色彩的节日。在台北近郊的北投照明寺和淡水

149

情人寺，每年七夕前后总是人声鼎沸，一对对情侣从各地涌向情人庙朝觐，立下海誓山盟。

（一）七夕食疗

各地乞巧风俗都表现了劳动人民想勤劳手巧、向织女学习劳动技能的强烈愿望。但是在台湾大部分地区，七夕独特的风俗是有趣的保健风俗，乞巧反不热闹。《台湾风物志》记载："中原妇女有乞巧之习。但台湾不产棉，妇女少问红事，且此月恰为全年农事最忙时，故台湾人不重七夕。"

台湾地区不重乞巧，但是在七夕尤重食疗保健。每到七夕之际，几乎家家户户要买来中药使君子和石榴。七夕这天晚餐，就用买来的使君子煮鸡蛋、瘦猪肉、猪小肠、螃蟹等，晚饭后分食石榴。这两种食物均有一定的驱虫功能，因而很受欢迎。说来有趣，台湾七夕的晚餐，民间还习惯煮食红糖干饭，这对诱虫吃药也起了辅助作用。因何有此独特节俗？相传出自海峡两岸尊奉的北宋名医"保生大帝"吴夲。景佑元年（1034 年）夏令，闽南一带瘟疫流行，好心的名医吴夲带着徒弟，四处采药救治百姓。他见许多大人小孩患有虫病，就倡导人们在七夕这天食用使君子、石榴。因七夕这天日子特殊，便于百姓记住，也正好是石榴成熟季节，民众都遵嘱去做，起到了意想不到的保健作用，于是后来便相沿成俗，并随着闽南移民至台湾而沿袭至今。由于吴夲医术高超，医德高尚，上自皇家，下至贫民，都尊崇他为"医神"。宋代乾道年间（1165—1173 年），皇上封他为"忠显侯"、"大道真人"。明成祖永乐十七年（1419 年），又追封吴夲为"医灵妙道真君"、"万寿无极保生大帝"。在台湾，祭祀保生大帝的庙宇竟多达 162 座。

○厦门青礁慈济宫里的保生大帝雕像

（二）"七娘妈"诞辰日

七夕节是"七娘妈"的诞辰日。七娘妈又称"七星妈"，是中国南方和台湾一半为保护孩子平安和健康的神。据闽南籍台湾学者林再复的《闽南人》一书考证，闽南人过去越峡跨洋到台湾地区或异国他邦经商、谋生，大都多年未能归，妇女们只好把所有的希望，都寄托在孩子身上，有了希望才有生活下去的勇气。所以，七夕这一相思传情的节日又演变成对保护孩子的"七娘妈"神的祈祷。

每年这天的中午，人们便要祭祀"七娘妈"。旧时人们要备瓜果菜肴七盘、胭脂花粉七件、剪刀七把、燃香七炷、酒杯七盏、筷子七双、纸轿七乘。热情好客的闽南人和台湾人，将"七娘妈"的六位姐姐也一并请来供奉了，所以贡品都是七份。这也与中国传统文化中对"数字"的崇拜。"数七"是阳刚之数，寓意吉祥天意。闽南和台湾人将"七"视为蒸蒸日上、积极奋发的吉祥数字，如"七上八下""七成八败"等。

这一天,台湾民间还流行一种"成人礼",即孩子长到满15岁时,父母领着他带着供品到七娘妈庙酬谢,答谢"七娘妈"保护孩子度过了幼年、童年和少年时代。在这一天,台南地区要为16岁的孩子"做十六岁",行成人礼。由双亲捧着特制的"七娘妈亭"(又称七星亭,一般用竹木和纸糊),立于神案前,年满16岁的子女由案下匍匐穿过,男孩起身后须往左绕三圈,称"出鸟母宫";女孩起身后须往右绕三圈,称"出婆妈"。如此完成,则意味着孩子已经长大成人。然后,再将"七娘妈亭"投入火中,奉献给七娘妈。有些人家,还由外婆家准备16岁仪式的衣服、手链、首饰、脚踏车等礼物。一些富庶的人家,除了"做十六岁"仪式、祭谢"七娘妈"之外,还专门为孩子举行成人礼的事而宴请亲友,庆贺一番。

当今台湾一些地方政府还每年举办"七夕十六岁艺术节",让身处现代文明的台湾人,还像古人一样度过一个浪漫、唯美、有意境的七夕节。

(三)七夕拜"床母"

台湾七夕拜七娘妈之外,往往也另备小碗油饭到房中拜"床母",二者有类似含义。生产、育儿,这都是女性的职责,因此这类神祇也都是女性神;在女性神与女性信徒之间,遂构成密切的联系,化解了女性在承担母职时的焦虑与恐惧。"床母"是儿童的保护神,七月七日是床母的生日,家中有儿童的家庭,在当天傍晚时,在儿童睡的床边拜床母。供品包括油饭、鸡酒(或麻油鸡),焚烧用的"四方金"和"床母衣"。拜床母时不宜太长,不像平常祭拜要斟酒三巡,大约供品摆好,香点了以后,就可以准备烧"四方金"和"床母衣",烧完即可撤供,希望孩子快快长大,不能拜太久,怕床母会宠孩子赖床等。

　　传统的七夕节俗文化是一种最具亲和力、人情味的文化。在同风同俗同方言的闽南和台湾地区，自古至今七夕节不但古风未泯，而且人们把这个节过得有情有味、多姿多彩，这是两岸血缘亲、俗缘深的节俗见证。

五、
七夕节在海外的传播

　　中国的七夕节形成已久，成为一种文化。七夕节不但在我国国内受到重视，它还作为一种文化传统走出了国门，在亚洲其他国家得以流传。

（一）七夕节在日本：和技艺相连，与爱情无关

　　中日两国一衣带水，自古以来联系就非常密切。古代日本人在创造本土文化的同时，不断地从先进的中国文化中吸取养分，滋养并发展日本本土文化。然而，文化的传承绝不是原封不动地代代照搬，随着历史的变迁，文化在不同地区的传播从内容到形式或多或少都会发生变化，甚至是剧烈的变化。日本在吸收中国文化时，为

○日本仙台的七夕祭

了使之适应自身的社会环境，对其进行了取舍与组装，然后世代传承。作为日本五大传统节日之一的七夕节，便是中国七夕节传入日本之后与本土文化融合而形成的实例。

日本的七夕节源自中国，延续了乞巧的风俗与习惯，现已成为日本民间重要的传统节日。七夕节在日本原来是农历七月初七，明治维新之后，日本废除了农历，所以现在日本的七夕节，是每年阳历七月七日。但是日本的七夕节与中国的七夕节有很大差异，日本的七夕节不是用来祈求爱情的，而是祈求少女们能拥有一身好手艺。

在七夕到来之前和当天，人们总要为它举办一些活动以示庆祝、纪念，如选美、马拉松、七夕舞会等。这一天是人们诉说心愿的日子，在日本有把自己的心愿写在彩纸上，或把它们挂在竹林中，或放入江河中，以此来祈求自己的愿望得以实现的习俗。这个习俗是从江户时代开始的。在临近七夕的日子里，很多地方都会有七夕竹子树，在商店卖服饰的地方、超市结款的地方都会设立七夕许愿树。在一些大型的庆祝典礼上还会举行竹饰大赛，由当地的幼儿园、小学等学校组织，创作各自的竹饰，并进行评比，选出最有特色的竹饰进行展示。

　　每年这个时候，大人和孩子都会聚在一起，在五颜六色的长条诗笺上写下愿望和诗歌，连同用纸做的装饰品一起挂在自家院内的小竹子上。此外还要在院子里摆上玉米、梨等供品，以此请求织女星保佑自家女孩的书法、裁衣等手艺能有所进步。庆典结束时，这些供品将被放到河里顺水漂走，以此象征着自己的心愿能够到达天河。

　　日本每个城市都用很高的扈的支柱插到土里，周围的人在纸上写下自己的心愿，然后折成细长条状，随便系上。有的城市会把纸张做成各种形状、各种颜色，吸引来宾参观。日本小孩子最喜欢过这个节日，在一个叫淡岛的地方还有姓七夕这个姓的人。

　　日本各地每年夏天还会举办一年一度的七夕祭。人们身穿传统服装，载歌载舞，欢天喜地，街头巷尾挤满了观看和游玩的大人、孩子。此外，配合七夕祭的还有每年夏季的烟花大会。这些都是日本七夕

○神奈川县平塚市热闹的七夕祭

155

节所特有的活动。日本的七夕节有很多活动，主要有歌舞表演、焰火、抬轿子等，非常热闹。最著名的地方是京都府的北野天满宫、香川县的金刀吡罗宫、神奈川县的平冢市和富山县的高冈市。

（二）七夕节在韩国：重祭祀，讲究饮食

　　韩国著名文学家崔南善在《朝鲜常识》中记载，七夕原来是中国的习俗，后传到了韩国，最初是在皇族、贵族中流行祭拜牵牛和织女星，后来慢慢在韩国民间流传开来。

　　韩国七夕最具代表性的风俗就是祈求织女星。女性通过祈求织女星希望自己与织女一样有着灵巧的手，织布织得更好。当天早晨女性把香瓜、黄瓜等瓜果放在桌子上磕头祈求，让自己织布的手艺越来越好。

　　韩国七夕的另一个重要事宜就是祭祀。祭祀可分为家庭祭祀和集体祭祀两种。韩国女性要在祭台上放干净的井水，牛郎、织女不是祭祀对象，主要是为了祈求亲朋好友的平安。有些地方则举行祈

○韩国七夕节的农乐表演

求丰收的田祭。

韩国的七夕饮食也有讲究，传统食品有面条、麦煎饼、蒸糕。

当然，一种文化由一个地域传另外一个地域，必然要与本土文化相融合，才能更有生命力，才能存活流传下去，七夕节在日本、韩国等国的流传就是这样。流传在外的七夕节，一方面必然体现华夏民族的文化，表现出中华民族文化的传承意义；另一方面，是中华民族文化与他国文化的融合。

Chapter Three
Spreading of Double Seventh Festival

Double Seventh Day is one of the most romantic and popular Chinese traditional festivals. And it was especially in vogue during the Tang and Song Dynasties. However, the trend of celebrating Double Seventh Festival underwent gradual declination since then, and the tradition was inherited mainly in southwestern China, such as Guangdong and Fujian Provinces. In modern times, the festival endowed with humanist and romantic color has been revitalized with people's efforts on its renewal, revealing an everlasting force of life. Due to a vast territory and colorful regional cultures of China, rituals of celebrating Double Seventh Day vary in different places. Taking Shandong Province in the north, Guangdong Province in the south, Hakka people and Taiwan districts as examples, this chapter tries to introduce the spreading of Double Seventh Festival in China from an overall point of view.

1. Double Seventh Festival in Shandong Province

Shandong Province has celebrated Double Seventh Festival since old times, holding various activities of Skill Praying. People usually look up to the sky on that night, trying to see if the Cowherd and the Weaving Maid are meeting above the Heaven River; they also hide in the grape trellis, trying to overhear the whispers of the couple in dating. Admiring the skillful handicraft of the Weaving Maid, girls would offer fresh vegetables and fruits for worship on that day, praying that the Weaving Maid could bless them with clever mind and skillful hands.

Shandong Province pays much attention to this holiday, with various activities of Skill Praying popular in various areas, forming a complete chain of Double Seventh Culture.

Heze County, Shandong Province: Making Jiaozi, Whispers under the Grape Trellis, and Rain of Lovesickness by the Weaving Maid

There is a special activity of Skill Praying in Heze County of Shandong Province – making Jiaozi. On Double Seventh Day, unmarried young girls could take part in the activity in groups of seven. It is said that on that night these young girls would put on beautiful clothes and make Jiaozi with the filling containing seven kinds of flowers. In addition, seven needles would be wrapped into some of the Jiaozi. Later, the girls would eat the cooked Jiaozi together, and if someone bites the point of a needle, it means she would be blessed with clever hands and good marriage; on the other hand, if she bites the eye of a needle, it means she would not have skillful handicraft. In the end, the one biting most needle tips is considered the cleverest girl.

159

According to the folklore, hiding under the grape trellis, people can hear the whispers of the Cowherd and the Weaving Maid on the third watch of the night (i.e. from 11:00 pm to 1:00 am) of Double Seventh Festival, so some curious boys and girls often follow this custom to check the truth of the saying. Among the local elders there spreads such a belief: on The night of Double Seventh Festival, one could hear the whispers under the grape trellis, but if one look up at the sky, he would see two fireballs colliding, then he would become blind, deserving the punishment for offending the heaven immortals by seeing something unrightfully. This is superstitious yet interesting indeed. Another belief is that the morning of Double Seventh Day would be extremely quiet with no magpie in vision, as magpies must hasten to the faraway Heaven River to build bridge for the Cowherd and the Weaving Maid. Still another saying is that it will surely rain on Double Seventh Day, and that means the Cowherd and the Weaving Maid are crying. As the couple are allowed to see each other just once a year, their meeting is sad with lots of tears. People call the rain on Double Seventh Day as "Rain of Lovesickness" or "Tears of Lovesickness".

Qufu City, Shandong Province: Making Skill Lanterns, Washing Hair and Airing Clothes

In Qufu City of Shandong Province there is the tradition of making Skill Snacks and Skill Lanterns in different styles. Girls make flour into Skill Snacks – pancakes with different designs of flowers such as lotus flower, peony, chrysanthemum, Chinese rose, herba peony, fingered citron, hosta, orchid, begonia, magnolia, plum flower, etc. While the designs of Skill Lanterns tells vividly traditional stories and legends, including

160

Eight Immortals Crossing the Sea, Immortals Celebrating the Birthday of Queen Mother, A Lad Worshipping Avalokitesvara, Three Immortals of Fortune, Wealth, and *Longevity,* and so on. It is said that Skill Snacks and Skill Lanterns would be sent as holiday gifts from the Confucius Family Mansion to the families of their relatives and friends. On the night of Double Seventh Festival, Skill Snacks and Skill Lanterns would be laid out first at the gate of Confucius Family Mansion, then before each gate from Zhongyi Road to Houtang Tower, as well as on all garden roads and scenic spots. People of every household would sit in the courtyard at night, gazing upon the starry sky for the meeting of the Cowherd and the Weaving Maid. People from Qufu City of Shandong also develop the habit of washing hair and airing clothes on Double Seventh Day, as saying has it that if a girl wash hair on this day, her hair would become lustrous and soft, smelling pleasant.

Jiaodong District, Shandong Province: Stealing Green Sorghum Stalk

In Jiaodong District of Shandong Province there is the custom of "Inviting the Weaving Maid" before Skill Praying. Girls would "steal" some green sorghum stalks from fields at daytime, without looking back or speaking on the way home, then set up a niche with the stalks or put the stalks on a mound to lay the picture of the Weaving Maid. At night, girls would walk around the well platform for one circle with some stalks in hand, inviting the Weaving Maid to descend to her niche. Then they usually sit before the picture of the Weaving Maid to pray for the skill. Girls usually sing a ballad while clapping their hands: "One clap brings the Double First Day, the Weaving Maid teaches me to sew shoe soles; two claps bring the Double Second Day, she teaches me to embroider the dress with flowers..." They continue singing until the part on the Double Twelfth Day finished.

Rongcheng City, Shandong Province: Planting "Skill Vegetable" and Making "Skill Flower"

In Rongcheng City of Shandong Province, there are two customary activities: one is planting "Skill Vegetable", which is actually wheat sprouts bred in the vat; the other is making "Skill Flower", which is actually food made of flour with designs of flowers. In other places of Shangdong Province such as Jinan, Huimin and Gaoqing, activities of Skill Praying are comparatively simpler. People just lay out fruits, and if spiders spin web on the fruits, they take it as a sign of getting skill. While in counties like Juancheng, Caoxian, Pingyuan, there is an interesting activity of Skill Praying called having "Skill Meal": Seven girls would make Jiaozi together, three of which containing a coin, a needle and a red date in the filling respectively; they would eat the Jiaozi after Skill Praying, and according to the old saying, anyone who comes across the coin would get fortune, the needle, skill, and the red date, marriage.

Other Places of Shandong Province: Skill Competition and Planting Skill Sprouts

Records of Ji'nan City in the Kangxi Period of Qing Dynasty reads that: "On Double Seventh Day, women usually lay out fruits in the courtyard, festoon buildings and thread needles for Skill Praying. And they hold that skill-praying activities work if the melon is covered by spider web."The night of Double Seventh Festival is often bustling with skill-praying activities. Girls wearing new clothes gather in groups in the courtyard, and set out the sacrificial table with fruits and cosmetics laid, worshiping the Weaving Maid while singing, "Holy heaven and earth! We sincerely invite the Weaving Maid to descend from sky! We do not intend to acquire Her needle or thread, but to learn Her great skill in needlecraft!" In addition, two kinds of activity are popular in some places–"Threading Needle for Skill Praying" and "Floating Needle for

Love Token on Double Seventh Day: Ball Made of Strips of Silk

Skill Praying". The former one is inserting the sesame sprout or thread through a needle or a special seven-eye needle by the faint light of burning incense, and who does successfully and quickly would get the skill in handicraft; the latter is floating a needle or a corn sprout on the water in a bowl which has been put in the sunlight for a whole morning, and the shape of the shadow under the water is observed as the sign of getting the skill or not. Usually, if the shadow appears to be too thick and straight, or slight and thin, it means Skill Praying fails.

Skill-praying activities in Shandong Province are similar to contests, just like the Skill Competition in ancient times. The contemporary activities such as threading needles, steaming Skill Breads, making Skill Snacks, planting Skill Sprouts and making handiwork of dough, paper-cut or embroidery are all evolved from ancient customs of Skill Competition. Changdao County used to hold activities of Skill Competition. Before the festival, girls gathered to decorate the Skill Shed, exhibiting such kinds of handiwork as lion, fighting cock, phoenix, carp jumping over the dragon gate, spinning lantern, golden clock, pastry, etc. Then on the festival night, girls gathered in the Skill Shed after supper, lit the lamp or candle, and sang songs for Skill Praying. Their performance usually attracted a lot of audience and would last for about four days, sometimes shown in different villages. In some counties like Wuli and Changdao there are customs of planting Skill Sprouts and seeing Skill Clouds. The shepherd boy in Wuli always pick wild flowers on Double Seventh Day and hang them on bull's horn as a "celebration of bull's birthday", as this day is said to be bull's birthday.

Typical food on Skill Praying Day in Shandong includes

noodle, Jiaozi, steamed buns, baked pastries, etc. People from Linyi make noodle using stored dew; people from Cangyi make "Cloud Noodle" on this day, implying the Skill Cloud; people from Changyi steam stuffed bun with seven wild vegetables in the filling; and people from Jiaodong often bake "Skill Pastries" (first mixing the dough with oil, egg, and sugar, then making it into pastries of different designs such as lotus flower, peach, or fish, baking them), string the pastries to hang on children's necks as snacks of playtime, or send the pastries to relatives and friends as a gift.

2. Double Seventh Festival in Guangdong Province

Double Seventh Day is the most romantic traditional festival in China, valued greatly by girls. In contrast with the customs of eating Skill Snacks and Jiaozi, people in south of the Five Ridges of China have their unique ways of celebrating: praying to the Weaving Maid, celebrating the birthday of the Weaving Maid, fetching water on Double Seventh Day, dying fingernails...

Guangdong Province: Seven Girls' Meeting

In Guangdong, Double Seventh Festival was valued most in historical periods of the Qing Dynasty and the Republic of China. Qu Dajun had recorded in his book A New Account of Guangdong the splendid situation of "Seven Girls' Meeting" in the early Qing Dynasty, which was also called "Praying to the Weaving Maid" in folk. Many intersting customs were passed down to the period of the Republic of China.

The event of "Praying to the Weaving Maid" was generally organized by girls and young wives (while men and elder women could just observe the ceremony and do the worship later). As early as in the sixth lunar month, a dozen of girls began to prepare the event by putting corns, wheats, mung beans in the bowls full of water, waiting them to sprout. As Double Seventh Day was approaching, the girls were busier. They must raise money, and with the help of their families, they would make various handicrafts from bamboo strips or paper, including the Magpie Bridge.

On the night of Double Seventh Day, girls laid out a square table in the hall, covered it with embroidered table cloth, and displayed all kinds of flowers, fruits and handicrafts, exhibiting their skills in all possible means. There was the plate of corn sprouts or bean sprouts surrounded with red paper slips, with a lamp in the middle of the plate and thin painting around the lamp, appearing so beautiful with blurring light glowing out of the painting. There was the bronze or china vase with flowers arraged delicately in it, fragrance of magnolia, jasmine and other flowers wafting in the air. There was the pot inserted with artificial and real flowers, lotus flower, rose, lily, and camellia blooming together, difficult for one to recognize which is genuine and which is sham. And there was the amazing fruit tray, with fruits like apples, peaches, persimmon, etc. vividly carved and piled into shapes of birds or beasts. Then, you could find embroidered mini objects, such as clothes, dresses, sockes and shoes, tents, sheets, curtains, table cloths, fans, handkerchieves, some about one inch long, some just the size of a fingernail. And mini constructions of pavilions and towers are delicate and skillful in design, with corn and bean sprouts growing out of the soil on small wood slats. Girls also made rice grains, sesames, rushes, colorful papers into tables, chairs, bottles, ovens, flowers, fruits and stationery aritcles, and piled beans of different textures into various sacrifical objects. Besides, there were lanterns of different shapes, made from glass, paper, grapefruit skin, and eggshell. Dolls of colorful silk fabrics made by girls were most beautiful and pleasing, with the Cowherd, the Weaving Maid and two children on the upper layer, and music instrument players on the lower layer celebrating the family reunion. Other figures from plays like "Romance of the Western Chamber", "A Dream in Red Mansions", or "Generals of the Yang Family" were also displayed among dolls. Of course, cosmetic supplies were never missing, and such things as rouge box, mirror, comb, velvet flower, face powder were offerd to the Weaving Maid as well as to girls themselves. Some wax fruits and animals were just lovely. In addtition, there were foods like sweet and savoury snacks, tea, wine, melon seeds, peanuts. Last but not least, there must be candlesticks with candles lit, and incense burners with best sanders in them.

Girls would dress themselves up elaborately on the night of Double Seventh Festival, washing their hair and having baths with water of the Heaven River, putting on silk dresses or Qipao, wearing magnolias or jasmines on their hair buns, applying cosmetics on their faces, and dying fingernails with the dew of impatiens. After dressing up, girls sat down around the square table and began their games. Some made poems and couplets, some played wager games and guessed riddles, some threaded needle for Skill Praying, some told stories and allusions about the Cowherd and the Weaving Maid, some invited performers to sing opera of Guangdong and play music, and some play musical instruments themselves. People could also walk around to visit the sacrifical tables of different families, and the hostess would be pleased to treat all guests. When it was twelve o'clock, the lucky hour for the Weaving Maid to descend to the mortal world, all lamps, incense and candles would be lit up. In the glorious light and jubilant atmosphere, girls happily thread needles and welcome the Weaving Maid. People didn't disperse until they finished a banquet held in the end. The occasion was vividly described in a poem of Qing Dynasty – *Zhuzhi Poem on Double Seventh Day of Guangzhou*:

> Jade gates of embroidery compounds opened one another,
> With screens of flowers and terraces of jasper.
> Girls of Green Brook and sisters of Blue Bridge,
> Gathered to keep an appointment this night for Skill Praying.

Guangzhou City: "Welcoming Immortals" on Double Seventh Day

The Skill Praying Festival has its own features in Guangzhou City. Before the festival, girls often make various handicrafts with colorful papers, rushes, cords and so on; and they put corns or mung beans in a small box filled with water, which will be offered as sacrifices for worshiping when sprouts of two inches or so come out of the water, and the activity is called "Praying with Immortal Crops" or "Praying with Holy Vegetables".

Before the arrival of the festival, girls would have prepared various novel objects, such as models of flowers, fruits, court ladies, containers, palaces, etc. made of materials like rushes, colorful papers, sesames, rice grains, and so on. They also put corns and mung beans in small boxes filled with water, which would be offered as sacrifices for worshiping when sprouts

"Welcoming Immortals" on Double Seventh Day

of two inches or so come out of the water, and the ritual is called "Praying With Immortal Crops" or "Praying with Holy Vegetables". On the sixth and seventh night of the seventh lunar month, girls would dress themselves up with beautiful clothes and jewels, paint their nails red, and put various objects prepared beforehand (such as antiques, flowers, fruits, rouge and powder) onto the sacrificial table in the living room. An oil lamp was usually put in the middle between "Immortal Corns" or "Holy Vegetables". At that time, the living rooms of well-off families were often decorated luxuriously, while common families tried their best to make the living room tidy.

Having prepared everything, girls would light up incense and candles, and pray to the starry sky. This ritual was called "Welcoming Immortals". They would worship for seven times from the third watch to the fifth watch at night (i.e. from 11:00 pm to 5:00 am). In addition to inviting relatives and friends to home, they invited familiar (or unfamiliar) girls in the neighborhood to pray to the immortal together, and to appreciate handicrafts and toys. Boisterous atmosphere made everyone happy. The more praises the handicrafts and toys got from the guests, the more pleased and honored the hostess would feel. Girls of Guangzhou City took it as a rare chance to show their skill and handicraft in public.

After worshipping, girls would insert colorful threads into needles by lamps (which was called "Learning the Skill of Using Gold Needle from the Weaving Maid"), and anyone successfully threaded seven needles would be addressed as a "flexible hand" (granted with skill), otherwise it meant she failed to get the skill. The occasion was written into one Tang poem:

"It is not threading the needle in moonlight that is hard
But handling the thread properly against the wind.
If you wonder who has been granted with skill?
Check and find it out in the following morning."

Next, girls would burn the paper cosmetic boxes containing paper clothes, shoes, rough and powder, mirrors, of such and such, everything prepared in sevenfold. After the sacrificial ceremony, things would continue being exhibited on the sacrificial table for girls' comments when they visited different homes the next day. It is recorded on the books of the Ming Dynasty, the Qing Dynasty and the Republic of China

Offerings like tea cups and fruits laid out on the sacrificial table

that, handicrafts exhibited by girls of Guangzhou included: embroidered shoes in the size of a grain, fans in the size of a fingernail, mini elegant curtains of thin silk, artificial flowers of lotus, jasmine, rose and lily, and the flower pot in the size of a small wine glass holding both a genuine and an identical sham flower. On the night of Double Seventh Day, sacrificial ceremony continued and the Cowherd was to be worshipped this time, and mostly the ceremony was held by a boy. After Double Seventh Festival, girls sent their handicrafts to each other as a token of friendship.

In Guangzhou, married women usually are not allowed to attend the immortal-worshiping ceremony on Double Seventh Day, instead, they would hold a "Farewell to Immortals" ceremony on the first Double Seventh Festival after their marriage. On the previous night of Double Seventh Day, newly married wives set out the sacrificial table to worship gods, they laid out animal sacrifices, red egg and dates. Also put on the

171

table are pears, signifying that daughters after their marriage would part with this girls' festival, because the two Chinese characters "pear" and "parting" pronounce in the same way.

Records of Guangzhou City has it that, on Double Seventh Day girls used to row boats near Chenxiangpu island of Shimen county. Their boats were named flower boats, usually decorated with jasmines, and it was believed that fairies would have a shower on this day. As the water of Shimen was very limpid, and lights of sunrise and sunset shone upon two mountains, sometimes visionary phantom appeared in the sky, which all girls went boating hoped to be lucky enough to see. Therefore, visiting Chenxiangpu island of Shimen county by boat became an important custom for the festival.

Chaoshan Area, Guangdong Province: "Going out of Garden" Ceremony on Double Seventh Festival

On Double Seventh Day, many families in Chaoshan Area will hold the ceremony "Going out of Garden" for their children aged 15, which is in fact a special coming-of-age ceremony.

Why is it called "Going out of Garden"? Older generations of Chaoshan Area think that children under 15 years old usually play in the garden, while if they come of age, they should go out of the garden and brave the storm of outer world. Natives of Chaoshan Area believe that Double Seventh Day is the birthday for "Gods Grandma and Grandpa", therefore hold the ceremony on that day to show gratitude for the two gods. Even many children in alien places would return to their hometowns for the "Going out of Garden" Ceremony at the age of 15, celebrating their birthday with relatives and friends.

On the early morning of Double Seventh Day, all dressed up for his "Going out of Garden" Ceremony, the child would first go up to mountain to worship Local God of the Land with his parents, who usually carry two full baskets of sacrificial offerings, then they would go back to the village to worshiop "Gods Grandma and Grandpa". The parents would prepare a sacrificial room for the ceremony, with Songs of Advising the World hanging on the wall for the child to read. When it is noon, relatives and friends all come to have dinner together. A special dish "pig's innards" is often served on the table, including pig's heart, liver and intestines, which, according to local sayings, symbolizes that the child has changed his innards and grown up into an adult.

In the past in this region, a child would not be treated as a real adult unless he celebrated his fifteenth birthday and his "Going out of Garden" Ceremony. Therefore, the ceremony used to be held in a formal way to suggest the child that he had grown up, while new clothes and shoes meant he had departed from the old years and entered adulthood.

In recent years, "Going out of Garden" Ceremony has become much simplified in Chaoshan Area due to the influence of modern trend. For example, clogs used to be worn in the ceremony is replaced with common shoes. Fortunately, the ceremony has been passed from generation to generation, and been maintained as an intangible cultural heritage.

3. Skill Praying Festival of Hakka People

Hakka people were originally Han people whose ancestral home was the Central Plain area. After five large-scale southward migrations, they became the Hakkas scattering in southern provinces of China with unique features. Hakka belongs to one of the eight important sub-ethnicities of Han and is estimated to have a population of 80 million. Hakka people have lived in southern China for more than 2000 years, distributed mainly in south Jiangxi Province, west Fujian Province and east Guangdong Province. The so-called "Hakka Four Cities" refers to Maizhou and Huizhou of Guangdong, Ganzhou of Jiangxi and Tingzhou of Fujian.

Skill Praying Festival in Hakka Homeland

In Hakka homeland of Ninghua County, Fujian Province, there are customs of "Skill Worshiping" and "Eating Seven-Layer Cake" on Skill Praying Festival, which, however, rarely known by outsiders.

On the sixth or seventh lunar month, everyone begins to make preparation for "Skill Worshiping" by making "Skill Sister Shoes". First, they draw on paper with color pens pictures of auspicious patterns, such as "Champion Scholar Worshipping Pagoda", "Fish Leaping over Dragon Gate", "Four Treasures of the Study", etc. Secondly, they cut out various flower patterns below the pictures to show their ingenuity. Thirdly, they hang underneath the picture a small shoe snipped out of red paper, which could be a boy's with a round toe cap, or a girl's with a pointed toe cap. Ready-made "Skill Sister Shoes" would be hung high in the newly-cut bamboo branches for people to watch. On Double Seventh Day, every family would set up decorated tent, draw colorful pictures and practice "Skill Calligraphy". Children are cheerful wit new wear, "tiger hat" on their heads which is hand-sewn by women, looking like a tiger head with two tiger ears and embroidered tiger mouth and beard, and "official boots" on their feet which are made imitating the style of ancient official boots. Fathers take their sons to the Confucius Temple to worship Confucius before his memorial tablet, which is called "Skill Worshipping". It is said that children who go to worship Confucius on this day would become smarter in study and be a promising official in future. For "Skill Worshiping", children light up incense and candle, present sacrificial offerings, and kneel down to kowtow. Fathers accompanying by also pray in murmur, to the effect that the children would become more intelligent and hard-working. Some children would recite an excerpt from Three-Character Classic or Analects of Confucius before the memorial tablet.

At night, children first kneel before the censer table to worship the Star of Cowherd and the Star of Weaving Maid, praying to be bestowed with wisdom. Then they recite the "Skill Praying Poem" under the guidance of adults, and write the poem on red paper with writing brush. The content of the poem varies with the age of the child. For example, younger children may recite:

"People celebrate the good night on Double Seventh Day

While double stars are meeting on the Magpie Bridge.

We children are pious in Skill Praying

Wishing a success in the Imperial Examination. "

While older ones may recite:

"The Cowherd and the Weaving Maid meet across the Heaven River;

That is why tonight is especially bright.

Every household sets up heavily decorated archway;

Everywhere chanting of poems is heard.

Piously I worship for a touch of Skill

Praying to get championship in the Imperial Examination."

Having written the poem, the children should sign their names and the date in a polite and formal manner in the bottom of paper. They should chant their poems repeatedly tlil the midnight when the Cowherd and the Weaving Maid meet, then they could burn their "Skill Praying Poems" in censers. Last, housewives serve out rice snacks in shapes of chicken, ducks, fishes or fruits, representing good luck and happiness, and the activity of "Skill Worshipping" does not end until children finish eating snacks and go to sleep.

Besides, there are customs of "Skill Triggering", "Skill Appreciating" and "Skill Applying" in Ninghua County. In the past, when girls are 16 years old, they were considered coming of age, and they must paint and cut seven pieces of "Skill Sister Shoes" with different patterns to show their ingenuity. When it was the Double Seventh Day before the girl's marriage, she would hold the ceremonies of "Skill Appreciating" and "Skill Applying", making twenty one pieces of "Skill Sister Shoes" with various and beautiful patterns, to impress her husband's family.

Another interesting and special custom is "Eating Seven-layer Cake", popular mainly among the She nationality in Zhiping county, northwest Fujian province. On the night of Double Seventh Day, every household would put fruits, tea, wine and Seven-Layer Cake on the table in the yard. Then all the family sit around the table, enjoying Seven-Layer Cake and moonlight, while the elderly telling the beautiful tale of the Cowherd and the Weaving Maid.

Cooking Seven-Layer Cake on Double Seventh Day is also a tradition in northwest Fujian province. Originally Seven-Layer Cake was made by Hakaa people in special honor of the

Seven-Layer Cake

day when the Cowherd and the Weaving Maid reunited. With time going by, it has gradually become a tradition for dwellers to make and eat Seven-Layer Cake. And families of engaged couples pay special attention to this tradition. Every Double Seventh Day, the family of fiance would send gifts to that of fiancée, including Seven-Layer Cake, similar to the tradition of sending New Year Cake in Spring Festival and Zongzi on Double Fifth Day. Having received the gifts, the family of fiancée usually cuts the Seven-Layer Cake into pieces and shares the cake with neighbors and relatives for the blessing of the couple.

There exists a close connection between the Seven-Layer Cake and the traditional culture of Double Seventh Day. Study Seven-Layer Cake carefully, and you will find that (the red color of) brown sugar symbolizes thriving and auspicious life, and (the white color of) refined sugar is the emblem of pure and noble character. Meanwhile, the cake consists of seven layers, corresponding in number with Double Seventh Day; and glutinous rice, a main ingredient of the cake, is of great stickiness, standing for the inseparable and unswerving love.

The Festival of Ancestors in Datian County

The seventh month of Chinese lunar calendar is nicknamed as "Melon Month", "Skill Month", and "Ghost Month", etc. It is called "Melon Month" probably for being the season of mellow fruits; while the names of "Skill Month" and "Ghost Month" are related to the folk culture of worshiping nature and ancestors.

Double Seventh Day is the time when the Cowherd and the Weaving Maid meet on the Magpie Bridge according to folk tales. During that night, many women usually practice needlework, pray to Vega (the Star of Weaving Maid) for skills, and hide under grape trellis to eavesdrop the whispers of love between the Cowherd and Weaving Maid. Therefore, the day is also called "Girls' Day" and "Lovers' Day". And the seventh lunar month in China is also called "Ghost Month" because the fifteenth of this month of is the Zhongyuan Festival of Taoism, which ranks as one of the three major Ghost Festivals in China, the other two being the Qingming Festival in the fourth lunar month and the Hanyi Festival in the tenth lunar month.

Chinese people, simple and honest, believe that everything on earth has its own soul. According to the record of Festival Law in *The Book of Rites*, "Anything exists on earth is called a life. While a creature's death is called a break, a human's death is called becoming a ghost." Since the Liang Dynasty, the Zhongyuan Festival has been observed in honor of ghosts among people. And here "ghosts" generally refer to their deceased ancestors. By all kinds of special worshipping ways, people cherish the memory of their ancestors and promote filial piety as a good Chinese tradition.

In Datian county, the seventh day of the seventh lunar month is the Ancestors' Day, and the 15th day of the month is called the Compensation Day, neither of which has anything to do with Skill Praying. From the first day of that month, all villagers around the county will go to repair roads with spontaneity, in unit of a village or a production team. Regardless of his family name and family size, each man of the village with nominal age between 18 and 50, should carry farm tools to weed, to ditch, to pad soil, to change bridge woods and so on. At that night, they would dine together after all those preparations for receiving ancestors back home to celebrate the festival.

Celebrating the festival is of great seriousness and filial piety. In the theory of Yin and Yang, the time from Wu hour (11:00 am-1:00 pm) to Hai hour (9:00 pm-11:00 pm) pertains to Yin, the activity time of some unseen things like gods and ghosts. Therefore, only after noon can every household take such offerings as pork, mutter, chicken, duck, rice cracker, fruits, and so forth, to ancestral shrine where venerable elders host the united worship. Then back home, each family would prepare for another copy of offerings for sacrifice. The worship in ancestral shrine usually contains the ritual of reading elegiac address, and even doing sacrificial ceremony by a wizard.

The Hui people in Shanchuan district celebrate the festival the earliest, beginning from the next day of repairing the roads, lasting until Compensation Day on the 15th. Actually, in addition to the main festival on the 7th, people in this region all celebrate the Compensation Day, which is specially prepared for the ancestors who cannot go back home in time to celebrate the main festival. It's said that on account of the rare population at that time, the ancestors together with people in Chuanshi, Huping, and nearby villages, hided themselves into the mountain from the brigands, and did not come back for the festival until brigands went away.

Belonging both to the Hakkas people and to the She nationality, the Wu family in Dongban would put off their celebration day to the 14th, of which the reason is unknown. The rule of their ancestors says that on the 14th people should butcher pig for worship and the pork can be distributed to every household after the ceremony. The pig is to be supplied by the family selected by drawing lots. Meanwhile, other families need to present three different kinds of food as offerings, which were appointed by the drawing lots of the previous year. All in all, their offerings for worship are of great variety.

Because of historical reasons, the land of Datian county was merged from nearby counties like Dehua, Zhangping, Yong'an, Youxi and so on when it was first set up in Ming Dynasty. People there found it hard to communicate in custom and language, as described in an old saying, "Different languages were used on two sides of a river; and different customs existed every five kilometers". Hence the special and vivid cultural phenomena of Datian came into being, with its district divided into Front Road, Back Road, High County, and Low County, while its language into Front Road dialect, Back Road dialect, Minnan dialect, Taoyuan dialect and Hakka dialect.

Along the districts of Guangping and Jianshe in Back Road,

deeply related to Youxi county, people also celebrate the festival on the fourteenth of the seventh lunar month. The Ancestors' Day in Back Road is actually Daughters' Day, which however does not mean a festival for unmarried daughters. Rather, married daughters should return home to give presents to their parents on that day. Back Road is so famous for its specialty "dried duck" that a dish of smoked duck or preserved duck is a must for the local dinner table on festivals, so dried duck and rice noodle are typical presents for parents from married daughters on this festival, similar to the custom of sending pig's legs and Zongzi to parents on Double Fifth Festival by married daughters in other areas. Of course, people in the districts of Guangping and Jianshe send gifts to parents on Double Fifth Festival as well, except for those living in the areas like Pingshan and Jiyang near to south Fujian Province.

The posterities of Chen clan who had settled in the Kuicheng area of Front Road before the first year of KaiCheng Period (836 A.D.), select the fifteenth of the seventh lunar month as the Ancestors' Day, the same day as the Zhongyuan Festival. And we don't know from whence they began to forbid sticky food such as sticky rice cake for sacrifice and offer only dry food to ancestors and spirits. It is said that offering with soup is a sign of disrespect, besides it is apt to be contaminated and become inedible after the sacrifice.

As described in *Records of Datian County* (the first edition in new China), on the 7th or 15th of seventh lunar month, commonly known as "Ghost Festival", families should prepare rice cakes and three animal sacrifices for ancestors. What's more, on the night of the 15th, people would insert incenses on the way from their doors down to roads. And children usually hold pomelos and dragons of straw inserted with many incense sticks, commonly known as "Pomelo Light" and "Straw Dragon". Then, there are water lamps set free under the bridge... People are doing all these activities to pray for harvest, peace and prosperity.

Though its date of celebration may vary in the seventh lunar month, Ancestors' Day is regarded important in Datian County, the causes of which have something to do with the season of fruit maturation, in addition to the cultural influence of traditional filial piety and Taoism. People of Datian County don't celebrate happy events in the sixth lunar month, unless it is unavoidable occasion like birthday, because this month, nicknamed as "Food Shortage Month", is a time when there is a food shortage between two harvests. While in the seventh lunar month, the fruits become ripe, and the chickens and ducks have grown up. With the coming of autumn and withering of grass, there is still a spare time from the harvests of rice and sweet potatoes. So it is not hard to understand that people choose such a time for Ancestors' Festival. They need to prepare for the harvest by mending road and eating something good. Besides, tomb-sweeping in Datian is usually arranged around the winter solstice, and people also have the habit of "Autumn Compensation"(i.e. to get used to season changing from summer to autumn, people would pay special attention to food so as to strike a balance). Thus, whether it is Melon Month or Ghost Month, there is some sense in the combination of the two.

Xianyou County, Fujian Province: Fried Soybeans and Peanuts with White Sugar

On this day in Xianyou county, every household will make

fried beans, with the ingredients of white sugar, soybeans and peanuts. The soybeans need soaking one day in advance and the next day they would be stir-fried half done for preparation. In the same way the peanuts would be stir-fried too. Then people melt the white sugar in the boiling pot, put the prepared soybeans and peanuts into the pot and boil them together. This custom has been alive for many years.

Meizhou City: Knotting Skillfully the Rice Straw

Meizhou City is located at the border region of Fujian, Guangdong and Jiangxi provinces, and it is the main habitation for the Hakka people. The cultural traditions of Hakka people, mostly brought by migrants from the Central China in the Tang and Song Dynasties, have blended well with the local custom.

As recorded in *Hakka Custom of Meizhou*, Hakka women of Meizhou follow the custom of "Threading needles for Skill Praying", which, after combining with the rice culture of Lingnan districts, has evolved into the custom of "Knotting Skillfully the Rice Straw". Firstly, ten long pieces of rice straw should be held in the middle by someone. Then a woman would knot every two pieces of straw together on both ends of the straw, with five knots on one end, and four knots on the other end. At last, unfold the straw, and see if these ten pieces of straw could be combined into a long piece by the knots. If they made it, that means the woman has been endowed with skill and she would have a smooth life in future.

4. Double Seventh Festival in Taiwan

Humane concern is best manifested in celebrations of Double Seventh Festival in Taiwan. The ancestors of many compatriots in Taiwan are the ancient immigrants of Fujian province, so Double Seventh Festival customs of these two areas are much the same, which in turn closes the distance between the two sides across the strait. In Taiwan, Double Seventh Festival, also called "Lovers' Day" or "Girls' Day", is the most romantic festival among eight major festivals in a year. On the outskirts of Taipei, Beitou Lighting Temple and Danshui Lovers' temple are bustling with people around Double Seventh Festival as couples from all around flock to the temples for their worship and make their vows of eternal love.

Diet Therapy on Double Seventh Festival

Customs of Skill Praying on Double Seventh Day in many places express the strong desire of diligent people to learn laboring skills from the Weaving Maid. However, in most areas of Taiwan, Skill Praying is not as popular as the unique and interesting custom of health care on Double Seventh Day. It is recorded in literature that "Women in Central Plains have the custom of Skill Praying, but Taiwanese pay little attention to it as Taiwan doesn't produce cotton and women seldom weave. Besides, the seventh lunar month is the busiest month of farming throughout the year."

Taiwan attaches little importance to Skill Praying, but pays abundant attention to diet health care. Around Double Seventh Day, almost every household would buy traditional Chinese medicine quisqualis and pomegranate, which are very popular for a certain function of expelling parasite. That night, they would cook quisqualis with eggs, lean pork, pig's intestine, crabs and so on for dinner, and eat pomegranate together after dinner. These two kinds of food are both effective in expelling parasites. Interesting enough, for the dinner of Double Seventh

Day in Taiwan, people are also used to cooking rice with brown sugar, which also played a fundamental role to expel parasite. Why is there such a special custom on this festival? It was said to be originated by Wu Yundong, "God of Life Protecting", a famous doctor in North Song Dynasty respected by people across the Taiwan Straits. That was the summer of Jingyou First Year (1034 A.D.), when there was an epidemic in the southern area of Fujian Province. Kind-hearted renowned doctor Wu Tao picked herbal medicines everywhere with his disciples, trying to cure afflicted people. Seeing that many adults and children got parasites in their bodies, he advised people to eat the fruit of Rangoon creeper and pomegranate on Double Seventh Day, as the date was easy to be kept in mind and pomegranate was mature around the time. Thus, people did as the doctor bid, and the advice did work. Hence the custom formed and was passed on with emigrants of south Fujian to Taiwan till today. Wu Tao was worshipped respectively as a God Doctor by all people for his superb medical skills and decent professional ethics. During the Qiandao Period of Song Dynasty(1165-1173), the emperor rewarded Wu Yundong with titles "Loyal Duke" and "Great Taoist". In the seventh year of Yongle Period of Ming Dynasty(1419), he was canonized as "Magic Doctor and Supreme Taoist" and "Immortal God of Life Protecting". There are as many as 162 temples for his sacrifice in Taiwan.

The Birthday of "Seventh Fairy Mom"

Double Seventh Day is also considered as the birthday of "Seventh Fairy Mom", who gets extensive folk worship for protecting children's safety and health. According to the study of south Fujian scholars, a lot of people from south Fujian used to cross Taiwan Strait to make a living in Taiwan or other foreign countries, yet without returning, therefore women left home had to put their hopes on their children for the courage of continuing life. And Double Seventh Day changed from a holiday of expressing love to that of praying to "Seventh Fairy Mom".

Every year of day, groups of people come to the temple of "Seventh Fairy Mom" to offer sacrificial flowers, fruits, domestic powder, animals, etc.

Every year on this day, people will sacrifice "Seventh Fairy Mom" at noon. In the old days, people used to prepare seven plates of fruits and dishes, seven pieces of rouge cosmetics, seven scissors, seven incense sticks, seven wineglasses, seven pairs of chopsticks, and seven paper sedans. The Taiwan people and People in southern Fujian are so hospitable that they also invited the six sisters of "Seventh Fairy Mom" for worship, therefore all the offerings are in seven shares. The custom is also related to the worship for number in traditional Chinese culture. "Seven" is the number of masculine nature, an auspicious symbol. Taiwan and south Fujian people regard "seven" as a thriving, positive lucky number, which explains such sayings as "seven is up and eight is down" and "seven means success, but eight means failure".

And on this day in Taiwan, there prevails an "Coming-of-Age Ceremony" – when the child reaches the age of 15, his parents would took him to the temple of "Seventh Fairy Mom" with sacrificial offerings, thanking "Seventh Fairy Mom" for protecting the child safely through his infantry, childhood and adolescence. While in Tainan City, "Coming-of-16 Ceremony" is popular for children. In addition to worship "Seventh Fairy

Mom" on this day, some parents would also invite relatives and friends to banquets, celebrating the "Coming-of-Age Ceremony" for children.

Today, some local governments in Taiwan still hold annual "Double Seventh Art Festival for Sixteen Years Olds", which enables modern Taiwan people to spend a romantic and beautiful Double Seventh Festival like their ancients.

Worshipping the Bed Mother in Taiwan

In addition to worshipping "Seventh Fairy Mother", Taiwan people also worship the Bed Mother with a small bowl of oil rice offered at home, and the two goddesses are considered to have similar duties and powers. Bearing and raising children are irreplaceable duties of women, so people usually worship goddesses to be in charge of this kind of things. Between goddesses and their female believers, a closer relationship can be formed to relieve the female of the anxiety and fear in the role of a mother. The Bed Mother is children' protection goddess, and her birthday is said to be on the Double Seventh Day. The families with children would worship her at the children' bedside in the evening, offering sacrifice such as oil rice and chicken wine (or sesame oil chicken), and burning the "quartet gold" and "clothes for the Bed Mother" made from paper. The time of worshiping should not be too long. Unlike the routine of pouring wine to worship for three times, people would burn the "quartet gold" and "clothes for the Bed Mother" right after presenting offerings and lighting incense. After that, they would remove the offering immediately, for they wish their children could grow up quickly, and they are afraid that if the worshipping lasts too long, the Bed Mother may spoil the children by allowing them get up too late.

The traditional Double Seventh Festival culture has a most attractive and humane nature. In Taiwan and south Fujian where same custom and same dialect exist, people not only keep well the tradition of celebrating this festival, but also endow it with moving humane colors. Double Seventh Festival is the evidence of affinity between people across the Strait.

5. Overseas Dissemination of Double Seventh Festival

The seventh day of the seventh lunar month is regarded as a traditional festival by the Han nationality of China. And it has a history so long that it has become a cultural symbol. Double Seventh Day is not only highly valued in China, but also popular in other Asian countries as a cultural tradition.

Double Seventh Festival in Japan: Related to Skill rather than to Love

China and Japan are close neighbors separated only by a strip of water, having developed intimate relationship since ancient times. When ancient Japanese were creating local culture, they absorbed nourishment constantly from China, thus enriched and developed their own culture. However, inheriting a culture is never copying. While it is spread in different districts, a culture will somewhat change in its content or form along with changes of history. In order to adapt to its own social environment, Japan made certain changes about Chinese culture while absorbing its essence, then passed it down from generation to generation. Japanese Tanabata Festival (i.e. Double Seventh Festival), is one of the five major traditional festivals in Japan, presenting a typical example of

The Scroll for Tanabata Festival in Sendai, Japan

cultural blending between Japan and China.

Tanabata Festival in Japan originated from China and has now become an important national festival carrying on the tradition of Skill Parying. The date of celebrating Tanabata used to be the same as in China, the seventh day of the seventh lunar month, but after the Meiji Restoration in Japan, the lunar calendar was abolished and the date of Tanabata was changed to be the seventh of July in solar calendar. In addition, Tanabata is different from Chinese Double Seventh Day in the purpose of celebration – in Japan the festival is not to pray for love, but for skills and ingenuity of girls.

Around Tanabata Festival, people always organize some activities for celebration and commemoration, such as beauty pageant, marathon, dancing party and so on. It is a day to express wishes. Ever since the Edo Period, Japanese people have followed the custom of writing wishes down on colorful papers, then hanging them on the bamboo or putting them into the river, to pray that their wishes can be fulfilled. When the festival is approaching, many places such as clothes stores or supermarkets will display bamboo wishing trees. In some big ceremonies there will be contests of bamboo decorations organized by local kindergartens and primary schools, etc. People usually make their bamboo decorations and compete with each other, selecting a few most distinctive items out for showcase.

In Japanese legends, the Weaving Maid would not only bless girls with skillful hands, but also satisfy their various dreams. In Chinese Double Seventh Festival girls pray for both skill and love, however, in Japanese Tanabata Festival girls pray for the former rather than the latter.

Every year at this time, adults and children will gather

Japanese Street Views on the Night of Tanabata Festival

together, writing wishes and poems in colorful strips, hanging them and other paper decorations on the bamboo in their own courtyards. In addition, people also lay out corn, pear and other offerings, praying that the Weaving Maid would bless their girls with progress in calligraphy, tailoring and other crafts. After the ceremony, these offerings will be put into the river to flow away, which symbolizes that their wishes could reach the Heaven River.

In every Japanese city, tall bamboo poles would be stuck into the soil on this day, and people around usually fold paper into a long and narrow strip with their wishes written on it and then tie it on bamboo branches. In some cities, people fold colorful paper into various shapes, drawing the attention of plenty visitors. Tanabata is Japanese children's favorite festival. And interestingly, Tanabata is even used as a family name for some people in Awashima, Japan.

Besides, the celebrating event "Tanabata Matsuri" is held every summer across Japan. People would wear traditional clothes dancing and singing, all in jubilations, and streets would be crowded with adults and children watching and visiting. Along with "Tanabata Maturi", there are also annual firework shows, another special activity in Japanese Tanabata Festival. Japanese Tanabata activities vary in form from place to place, mainly including dancing and singing performance, firework show, carrying sedan-chair and other exciting programs. Places most famous for colorful festival activities are Kitano Tenmangu in Kyoto Prefecture, Kotohiragu in Kagawa Prefecture, Hiratsuka City in Kanagawa Prefecture and Takaoka

City in Toyama Prefecture.

Double Seventh Festival in South Korea: Highlighting Worship and Food

The noted South Korean litterateur Cui Nanshan once introduced Double Seventh Festival in his book General Knowledge on South Korea. According to him, celebrating the festival was originally a traditional Chinese custom but later spread to South Korea. Royal families and nobles usually worshiped the Star of Cowherd (i.e. Altair) and the Star of Weaving Maid (i.e. Vega) on that day and officials could get their festival subsidies. Later, it became popular gradually among people from grass root to celebrate the festival.

In South Korea, the most representative custom on the festival is to pray to the Star of Weaving Maid (i.e. Vega), through which women wish to become a better weaver with dexterity. On that morning, women put musk melon, cucumber and other fruits on the table, then kowtow and pray for a better weaving skill. Another important activity of the holiday is worshipping, which consists of family worship and collective worship. South Korean women should put clear water on the altar, but different from Chinese custom, the Cowherd and the Weaving Maid no longer being their targets of worship and South Korean people mainly pray for the safety of their friends and families. Some places also hold the field worshipping ceremony to pray for harvest. In addition, people pay special attention to food on Double Seventh Festival, traditional food being noodles, wheat pancakes and steamed cakes.

When a culture spreads from one region to another, it must blend with local culture to maintain its vitality, which is why Double Seventh Festival survives in Japan and South Korea. The spreading of Double Seventh Festival abroad epitomizes the inheritance significance of Chinese national culture on the one hand, and represents the cultural fusion between China and other nations one the other hand.

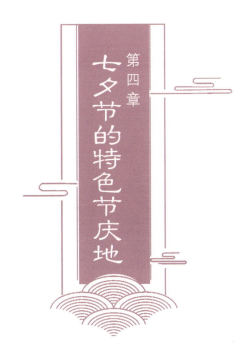

第四章
七夕节的特色节庆地

　　鹊桥相会是一个千古传颂的爱情故事，传说牛郎和织女每年农历七月初七这一天在天上鹊桥相会，七夕也被人们誉为"中国的情人节"。美丽的牛郎织女故事作为中国古代四大爱情悲剧之一，至今还没有确定的发源地。

一、
广东东莞：望牛墩"七夕贡案"

以"七夕贡案"闻名遐迩的广东省东莞市望牛墩镇的乞巧节，源自五代，历史悠久，虽然内容随着时代演进不断丰富，但依然保持着古朴风韵。每年农历七月初七的望牛墩七夕风情文化节，已被列入广东省非物质文化遗产名录，望牛墩镇也被授予"中国乞巧文化之乡"称号。

○ 望牛墩镇的七夕公园

望牛墩七夕风情文化节源于我国千年不朽的民间四大爱情故事传说之一——牛郎织女爱情故事传说。2004年以来，望牛墩镇立足于打造中国七夕文化名镇，以七夕文化为载体为平台，先后举办过五届大型七夕风情文化节，节日规模越来越大、特色越来越浓、影响越来越广。七夕风情文化节经过深入挖掘、精心打造，已从一个镇级活动上升为全国知名文化盛事，成为望牛墩镇享誉全国的一个独特文化符号，被誉为"群众艺术的节日、老百姓文化的盛会"。

（一）满载盛誉的望牛墩乞巧文化

2010年望牛墩七夕风情文化节被纳入"我们的节日"东莞市系列文化活动，以及由中国文化部、农业部等主办的"首届农民艺术节"系列活动。"七夕贡案"先后参加广东省首届非物质文化遗产保护成果展、广东省与东盟非物质文化遗产保护传承交流会、上海世博会"广东活动周"非物质文化遗产展等重大展览；2010年七夕贡案"仙凡缘"入选第十届中国民间文艺"山花奖"。

广东省博物馆、东莞市展览馆、东莞市非物质文化保护中心、东莞市饮食风俗博物馆都收藏有望牛墩镇的"七夕贡案"，七夕风情文化节的艺术魅力和社会影响力得到更广泛的传承和发展。

（二）望牛墩的名字起源

望牛墩是著名的中国乞巧文化之乡，也是广东省唯一一个以"牛"字命名的镇，并将"牛"作为全镇的象征和标志，与我国"牛郎织女"爱情故事神话传说是一种"天缘"，镇名的起源与"牛"有着千丝万缕的联系。关于望牛墩镇名的起源，社会上广泛流传着传说版和神话版两个版本。

传说版:《望牛墩镇志》记载，望牛墩始建于宋，原是东江支流下游的一片广阔滩涂，土壤肥沃，气候宜人，长着茂盛的牧草，是个天然好牧场，吸引周边的村民把牛群赶到滩涂上放牧。滩涂边有一块地势凸起的土墩，土墩上长着树木可以供村民乘凉休息，所以放牛的村民都习惯站在土墩上看牛群，随后该土墩被村民称为"望牛墩"。随着附近越来越多的村民迁徙到土墩居住，土墩地域开始慢慢扩张，进而演变成今天的望牛墩。

神话版: 在很久以前牛郎和织女在农历七月初七鹊桥相会，王母娘娘暗中派出两名天兵天将化身为一大一小老虎，围追堵截牛郎乘坐的神牛，阻止牛郎到天河与织女相会。神牛临危不惧，在将牛郎及其一对儿女安全送到银河鹊桥上后，力战两只老虎，搏斗中不幸负伤被迫四处奔跑躲闪，下到凡间。在途经一片水草茂盛的土墩时，神牛直奔而进并从此不见踪影，紧追不舍的一大一小两只老虎无可奈何，只好日夜蹲守在土墩周边。后来，神牛栖息的土墩就演变成今天的望牛墩，一大一小两只老虎就是今天虎门镇的大、小虎山。

（三）七夕贡案

每年乞巧节前，望牛墩镇的 21 个村都要准备好七夕贡案。乞巧节还没到，这里就热闹起来了。妇女们忙着准备摆放在祠堂贡案上的贡品，费尽心思地把贡案摆放得漂漂亮亮。传说乞巧节午夜，织女会带着 6 位姐姐踏过鹊桥，下凡到人间，来到贡案最漂亮的祠堂，与牛郎相会。多姿多彩的贡桌都摆放在各个祠堂大厅中间，贡桌上放着 7 只茶杯、7 样水果，每样水果都堆得像座小山。贡桌周围摆放着 7 种鲜花，花丛里放着一对大花瓶，花瓶里插着鲜艳的花枝，心灵手巧的妇女将这些花枝编成花桥。贡桌上摆着一对大红蜡烛，中间置放着一座金光闪闪的香炉。贡桌两旁摆放着 7 把红木椅，椅后挂着7 件不同颜色的古代服装。红木椅旁都摆着一张古化妆台，台上整齐地摆放木梳、发簪、胭脂等。摆放好一个贡案，少则需要一个星期，多则需要数月。少女、少妇们通过制作贡案展示自己的心灵手巧。

望牛墩七夕贡案主要有 3 种形式。一是家庭式，一家一户，以一张八仙台摆设；二是 7 家姐妹联合式，7 个姑娘共摆一台，多用 2 至 8 张八仙台摆设；三是全村集资合办。姑娘们在 10 多张八仙台上铺上大红布，摆上 7 种鲜花、7 种水果，摆满花花绿绿的饰物和神态活现的人物公仔等。

少女、少妇们用自己制作的巧物，祈求人神共赏，进而得到美满幸福的爱情婚姻。乞巧活动只在少女、少妇中进行，男子和老年妇女只能在旁观看。

到了七夕，贡案上得摆上茶酒斋饭、五谷杂粮，让七仙女下凡享用；还得摆上手工制作的可以舞动的龙、凤、狮，以贺乞巧节的到来；更以手工制作 7 种花、7 种果、7 双绣花鞋、7 张台椅、7 套衣服，

○望牛墩七夕风情文化节上人山人海

199

○七夕文化风情节上的微缩"龙舟"赛

　　"天上佳期逢七夕，人间乞巧拜双星。"乞巧节期间，望牛墩各村祠堂里挤满了人，不仅有来自广东各地的，还有从全国各地及海外慕名而来的。望牛墩乞巧节拜祭七姐的活动，按传统仪规进行，未婚女子和小孩才能前来拜祭，男孩拜祭牛郎、董永，女孩拜祭七仙女。拜祭时依序进行，年纪从小到大，一个接一个，拜祭的人要先喝口糖水，然后再用香浸过的水洗手，方能上前拜祭，拜祭时还要诚心诚意地三叩九拜。拜祭后，人们在祠堂里静静地坐着，等待派发物品。拜祭结束后，祠堂的长老会把贡案上的物品分派到每个拜祭人的手上。据说得到贡案上物品的人，都会得到七仙女的庇佑。

（四）望牛墩七夕风情文化节

　　每年七夕节前后，望牛墩都要在该镇文化广场举办盛大的七夕风情文化节。

　　在 2015 年 8 月举行的望牛墩镇第六届七夕风情文化节上，围绕

"浪漫七夕·幸福望溪"主题，先后举办了开幕式晚会、七夕文化论坛、特色贡案展览、七夕文化衍生产品展示会、历届七夕风情文化节活动花絮展览等7项活动。七夕当天，超过10万市民涌向望牛墩，大家从中尽情享受赏贡案、立盟誓、许情愿、渡鹊桥、观盛会的精彩文化盛宴，亲身体会七夕文化艺术奇葩的魅力和活力，体会七夕文化的艺术价值和社会价值。

最近一届的七夕风情文化节，是在2016年8月8日至10日举行的，依然吸引了近10万名市民前往观看。这一年的活动分为"相约望溪浪漫七夕会"、"相遇望溪民俗文化展"、"相爱望溪幸福大家秀"三大主题板块，既保留了大型七夕贡案展这个传统节目，还有爱的留恋·浪漫情缘会、爱的祈祷·荷灯祈福行、爱的味道·3D打印甜蜜美食秀、爱的盛宴·七夕祈福之夜、爱的记忆·水乡民俗风情展、爱的永恒·定格幸福照片征集、爱的旋律·经典情歌会等多项活动，精彩不停，浪漫不断。"七夕贡案"依然是2016年七夕风情节的重头戏，全镇21个村开展七夕贡案制作评比，展示了望牛墩民间乞巧贡案的盛景和精巧的技艺。

○一对情侣驻足望牛墩的"情缘墙"

旅游小贴士

望牛墩："中国乞巧文化之乡"

望牛墩镇位于广东省东莞市西部，始建于宋代，是一个具有800多年历史的小镇。这里土地肥沃，气候适宜，交通发达，素有"鱼米之乡"的美誉。

望牛墩镇有十多千米的河岸线，离广州新沙港、东莞虎门港也很近，是一个经济较发达的南方水乡特色小镇。

著名景点：

七夕文化公园、望牛墩龙舟文化体验区

最佳旅行时间：

4—6月、8—11月。

交通路线：

1.从广州机场或火车站，沿广深高速或沿江高速南行40千米，到达望牛墩镇。

2.从深圳宝安机场或深圳火车站，沿广深高速或沿江高速西北方向前行90千米，到达望牛墩镇。

二、
湖北郧西：七夕之城，爱在天河

　　湖北省郧西县地处湖北西北边陲，湖北陕西交界处，相传它是牛郎织女"七夕文化"的发源地，因为其很多地名、景点、传说、习俗都与牛郎织女故事非常吻合。

　　每年农历七月，人们仰望繁星密布的夜空，正东方有一颗星星特别耀眼明亮，这就是织女星。据专家研究，古代的七月是妇女织布的月份，故将这颗星定为织女星。古时八月，国家要挑选祭祀用

○天河七夕文化节开幕式

的牛，所以把这个月最亮的星星叫牵牛星。星象图上，浩瀚的银河系由北至南，东边是牛郎星，西边是织女星，中间隔着银河，两两相望不停地闪烁。在郧西县中部，有一条由北朝南流向的蜿蜒河流叫天河。天河发源于陕西，主要流经郧西境内。天河东边是杨家河、归仙河，西边是美女河、仙河，正好与天象对称。

郧西境内的天河，不仅在河名上与牛郎织女故事中的天河吻合，而且与天河流域的自然地貌和人文景观也有十分密切的联系。在天河流域，郧西县城东南边的石门

○《牛郎织女》特种邮票在天河首发

湾山上有一尊貌似女像的山石被称作"石婆婆"，在西北部的华盖山上也有一座似男人像的山峰被称作"石公公"。郧西人祖祖辈辈都认为这两块山石是牛郎、织女的化身。在天河上游的河中间有块兀立的巨石叫"金钗石"，传说是王母娘娘拔簪划天河时遗落在此的金簪化石。郧西县城西部的悬鼓公园里有一块如"悬鼓"的山石，传说是女娲炼石补天的石头，也有传说它是织女下凡洗浴时放置衣服的仙石。天河东面有一座海拔1069米的娘娘山，山顶的娘娘庙里供奉着王母娘娘的神像。

郧西县城西南悬鼓观东北方向的石梯子山上有一座尼姑庵，叫"天池庵"。很久以前，这里是香火旺盛的地方。一边是观一边是庵，一边是女一边是男。经考证，这一观一庵是淳朴的郧西人为了纪念牛郎、织女而修建的。

有天河，就有牛郎织女的传说，就有独特的七夕民俗。在郧西，

○ "天河作证"婚礼大典

人们将牛郎、织女忠贞不渝的爱情故事代代相传。老人时时告诫后辈：男儿要像牛郎一样勤劳、质朴、善良、执着，女儿要像织女一样智慧、忠贞、节俭、孝顺。在湖北西部有这样一种说法，"要吃大米到竹溪，要娶媳妇到郧西"。郧西是美女之乡，郧西女子的俊美、心善、手巧是人们公认的。专家认为，牛郎、织女确有其原型，后来演变成了神话故事。

在郧西天河流域广泛传承着穿针乞巧、投针验巧、贺牛生日、喜蛛应巧、拜魁星、葡萄架下听情话、祈福灯会、吃巧果等七夕习俗。每年农历七月初七，人们过"乞巧节"。那天，妇女们聚在一起开展各种劳动竞赛，以在竞赛中提高技艺。夜幕降临，人们来到河边燃放河灯。顺河漂流的盏盏河灯，寄托着人们对逝去亲人的哀思，承载着人们对家庭、亲人的祈福，同时也是在为牛郎指路，以助他尽快与织女相会。"河灯亮，河灯明，牛郎织女喜盈盈"的民谣，在郧西县境内广为流传。

"七"在郧西是个特别数字。婚俗中，有"七成八不成"之说，男方到女方家提亲，女方宴请男方客人，上七个菜，预示女方同意；上八个菜，则表示不同意这桩婚事。酒席上，人们划拳饮酒，通常用"七个巧"代表"七"。红白喜事，也与"七"有关。喜事要请七天假；丧事有七期，每期有七天。

郧西的民间小调和丧事孝歌里，也含有大量的有关牛郎织女的故事。郧西有完整的《牛郎织女》民歌，包括错传圣旨、牵牛游园、织女绣十针、花园相会、贬下凡间、牛郎遭难、兄弟分家、织女想四季、私下凡间、牛郎闹五更、老牛做媒、牛郎织女看花灯、织女怀胎、秋季尝新节、捉拿织女、鹊桥相会等章节。

近年来，郧西县实施"旅游立县"战略，以七夕文化为灵魂，以天河为轴心，全力打造七夕文化之乡，建设"婚旅之城、约会之乡、休闲之都"。在基础建设方面，已建成两个国家 4A 级景区"中国小九寨——五龙河"与"中国小雁荡——龙潭河"，正在规划建设"天河风景区"、天河口古镇和世界婚俗博览园；已经建成天河民俗博物馆、天河广场、七夕广场、七夕文化园、天河国际大酒店等系列七夕文化工程。

迄今，郧西县连续 6 年成功举办了"中国（郧西）·天河七夕文化节"。每年七夕节前后，天河织女形象大使评选、婚礼大典新人招募、郧西天河七夕文化歌曲征集、七夕文化研讨会、"天河作证"婚礼大典、专场文艺演出、嘉宾巡游五龙河等系列活动，通过主流媒体强势高调持续宣传，郧西七夕文化及节会的影响广为传播，郧西七夕文化旅游的人气大幅提升。与此同时，政府对在建的一批市政工程及路桥、建筑及景观进行了天河七夕文化的相关命名，企业抢注相关商标、命名相关商品、更换相关门牌、变更相关名称，让天河七夕元素及文化遍布郧西的各个角落，滋养着郧西人的思想和灵魂，影响着郧西人的生活方式和行为习惯，已经成为深入郧西人骨髓和血脉的文化自觉。

湖北郧西

郧西县人文历史悠久，旅游资源丰富，自然景观奇秀，是"中国七夕文化之乡""中国喜鹊之乡"。

郧西近年来以七夕文化为引领，把城区当景区建设，打造文化浓郁、生态宜居、宜游宜业的七夕之城。建设七夕广场、天河广场、七夕文化故事园等 10 处文化广场，在七夕广场建成时空隧道、世界第一铜牛、人造月亮、音乐喷泉等景观，形成"七夕文化大观园"；架起元春桥、望春桥、迎春桥等 12 座独具七夕文化特色的"春桥"；修建天河水体景观区，命名七夕大道、天河大道……城区路、桥、园、场、山、水等无不蕴含七夕元素。

著名景点：

五龙河风景区、龙潭河风景区、七夕天河广场、上津古镇等 4 个 4A 级景区

最佳旅行时间：

5 月至 10 月为宜，在每年七夕节前后一周举办的"七夕文化节"游玩更佳。

交通路线：

1.公路：福银高速（G70），自西安前往郧西约 240 千米，自湖北十堰前往约 70 千米。

2.机场：十堰武当山机场，距离郧西县城 80 千米，约 1 小时车程。

三、
广东连山："七月香"壮家戏水节

连山壮族瑶族自治县位于广东省西北部，粤湘桂三省（区）交界处，南至广州 265 千米，西邻桂林 300 千米。

传说每逢农历七月初七这一天，天上的"七仙女"姐妹在银河里沐浴嬉戏，午时前后，银河水与人间溪河水汇流，这天壮乡河里的水会变得特别清凉、干净，沐浴、饮用对人体健康十分有益。人

○广东连山壮乡梯田

们沐浴后，可消灾、除毒、驱邪，润肤丽体、少生疾病、延年益寿。因此，每逢此节，壮家人不分男女老幼齐聚到河里洗头、沐浴、耍水、嬉戏，祈求健康长寿、平安吉祥。在这一天取水制成的醋，醋香醇厚经久耐放。所以，这一天又被称为"七月香""女儿节""长久节"。

千百年来连山壮族都保持这种习俗，并演变成为壮族的一个盛大节日，"七月香"壮家戏水节因此演绎而来，并自 2006 年起在每年七夕这一天举办，将尘封多年的壮族传统文化再次呈现在世人面前。整个戏水节分为数个表演展示互动区：原生态歌舞实景演出、国家省市非遗展、民族民间艺术精品、壮瑶民族风情表演、戏水狂欢、壮瑶风味美食等，同时向游客观众奉上。

○ "七月香"壮家戏水节开幕式

50 米长的上吉路吉水壮瑶风情桥上铺着火红的地毯，两侧风雨走廊披挂着壮瑶风情图案，绣有壮瑶图腾的旌旗迎风猎猎作响。穿戴节日盛装的秀丽壮家阿妹为远道而来的客人戴上壮家绣球以示欢迎。霎时，壮家八音齐响，姑娘唱着欢快的迎客曲，将客人款款引向戏水舞台对面的嘉宾席。

国家级非物质文化遗产瑶族小长鼓舞、省级非物质文化遗产瑶

○广东连山壮家戏水节上的戏水狂欢

族八音悉数展示在河两岸的戏水通道上，许多分散各地各节日的文化艺术活动被同时搬上了艺术节的大舞台。千米文化长街浓缩了千年的壮瑶文化，令人目不暇接。

祭水祈福庄重审慎、戏水狂欢热烈奔放。河中的戏水舞台上，鼓声由慢而快，由弱渐强，狗牙旗队从舞台两侧呼啸而来，壮族师公口念祭语手舞铜铃走上主舞台，庄重祭水祈福……原生态歌舞上演，壮族山歌《客人来到咱壮乡》欢迎八方宾客，《耍水歌舞》欢快的音乐激发起两岸壮家小伙姑娘和游客强烈的戏水欲望。表演一结束，身着壮族服饰的 400 名姑娘、小伙从四面八方跃入吉水，泼水探情，戏水传意，男女欢歌。蜂拥而来的上万游客纷纷走向河中，加入壮家青年的戏水狂欢活动。

除了赏玩，壮瑶风味美食更令人嘴馋。戏水节期间独具壮乡民间风味的美食，如嫩滑爽口的壮家水浸白糍、垂涎欲滴的"拜散"腌肉、清香扑鼻的瑶家荷叶包……一款款深藏于大山的民族美食走上了美食殿堂。酒店、宾馆、小食铺纷纷打出民族招牌美食迎接各地游客。

多彩中国节

七夕节

游客们可在小桥流水河畔悠闲地品一品当地风味小吃，喝上两盅瑶家酿制的糯米红酒，清风徐来，不胜惬意。游客们除了可在美食节一饱口福外，还可在土特产一条街将未加工的当地土特产买回家，慢慢品味。

旅游小贴士

连山壮族瑶族自治县

作为全国唯一的壮族瑶族自治县和少数民族聚居区，连山有其独特的文化风情，闹年锣、抢铜锣、抢花炮、追天灯等。壮家的建筑、节日和婚俗都有着鲜明的民族特点。该县民族风情浓郁，已多年连续成功举办"七月香"壮家戏水节，壮瑶风情游独冠南粤。

旅游景点：

连山境内旅游资源丰富，有堪称"广东九寨沟"的大旭山瀑布群旅游区、"一脚踏三省"的鹰扬关景区、秀丽的两广界河风光、古朴幽静的福林苑、集亲水与健身于一体的淘金游、气象奇观"茅田云海"等。

最佳旅行时间：

11月至次年2月为宜。

交通路线：

1. 323国道，东接广东省韶关市，西连广西贺州市、柳州市，贯穿全境。

2. G55高速，二（连浩特）广（州）高速广东段连通粤湘桂三省区，

211

广州、深圳、长沙开车到连山都很方便。

3.航空，广州白云机场经二广高速车程为 2 小时。

四、
河北天河山：七夕情侣节

河北省邢台市是国家命名的中国七夕文化之乡、中国七夕文化研究基地。邢台天河山景区位于太行山深处，是牛郎织女故事的原生地，有大量的文化遗存和故事传说，2005 年在国家工商总局注册为"中国爱情山"。这里有着厚重、丰富的七夕文化。

河北省自从 2006 年 8 月开始，每年由政府有关部门牵头，在七夕节期间组织"七夕情侣节"，迄今已举办 11 届，在全国各地的七夕活动中甚为少见。河北省七夕情侣节先后于 2007 年和 2010 年在全国传统节日评奖中获奖，成为河北省的一个新的文化品牌，为全国打造"我们的节日"、弘扬中华传统文化做出了有益尝试。11 届七夕情侣节均在邢台天河山景区举办。

每年活动期间，经常出现"万人过七夕"的盛况。民间水陆婚俗表演、万人鹊桥会、邢台地方民俗文艺汇演及纺织工艺表演等特色活动同期举办，京津冀"非遗"民俗文化也登台展示。来自北京、

○河北天河山的标志性景点："牛郎织女"石刻

天津、河北等地区的非遗项目参展，呈现"非遗"民俗文化多彩风景线。通过传统民间工艺品展示，产品和古代爱情故事相结合，让游客更全面深入地了解牛郎织女爱情故事的美丽传说。

　　传统婚俗表演是七夕情侣节的一大亮点，不仅能让游客享受别样的视觉盛宴，而且能让游客在思想上对传统爱情文化有更直观的认识。活动组委会邀请专家查证资料、深入研究，组织景区员工对汉代水陆婚俗表演进行重新编排，在节日期间通过演出向游客再现原汁原味的古代爱情文化。前几届还评选了"恩爱夫妻·和谐家庭"，在群众中产生了强烈反响，起到了典型示范作用。

　　2015 年的七夕情侣节活动延续整整一周，期间，举办了"爱情1+1"FM896 万人相亲会，以电台为媒介，以文化节为背景，面向省内外邀请单身男女赴会；还举办了地方民俗文艺汇演和邢台民间手工艺、纺织工艺表演及产品展销，"回味经典、致敬爱情"民间水陆婚俗表演，"high 翻七夕"燕京啤酒音乐节。这些活动，既具有一定的展示性，也有很强的参与性，在为人们展示古代、现代爱情文化的同时，也让游客们有机会能真正体验到不一样的七夕节。

2016年的七夕情侣节，举办了"寻找今日织女星"、婚爱主题创作、主题歌曲演唱会、织女星典型经验交流会和七夕文化高层论坛等五大系列活动。"寻找今日织女星"评选采取单位申报和网上报名相结合的方式在河北省内评选基层"巧女、才女、孝女、善女"。七夕原本是属于劳动女性的节日，织女作为劳动女性的代表，是勤劳、美丽、贤惠、质朴、智慧、勇敢等优秀品质的代名词。她和牛郎男耕女织，共同劳动，夫妻恩爱，家庭和谐，用劳动创造了幸福生活。因此，"寻找今日织女星"也就是寻找当代的优秀新女性，借助这一活动寻找到优秀的现代"织女星"，宣传她们的优秀事迹，扶持她们的劳动事业，鼓励广大女性自强自立，更多地投入美好社会的建设中来。

旅游小贴士

天河山：中国爱情山

天河山位于河北省邢台市邢台县白岸乡清泉村，是中国七夕文化之乡，传说是牛郎织女传说的原生地。天河山屹立在晋冀交界处的太行山最绿的地方，总面积30平方千米。这里奇峰林立，峡谷幽峻，植被丰茂，林木葱郁；群瀑飞雪，清泉鸣筝，水源丰沛，是著名的"太行水乡"；松涛阵阵，牛羊成群，又被称为"云顶草原"。

天河山一带广泛流传着牛郎织女的故事，并拥有大量的文化遗存。2005年，天河山在国家工商总局注册为"中国爱情山"。2006年，天河山被命名为"中国七夕文化之乡"。

天河山风景区是国家4A级景区，国家重点风景名胜区、国家地质公园。人到这里，时如神游江南、时如梦游塞外、时如魂赴林海、时如足踏蓬莱。天河山以水叫绝,素以"五步一瀑,十步一潭"而著称。

文化活动:

1. 爱情文化节

每年七夕,天河山都会举办"七夕爱情文化节",借助牛郎织女的神话传说,展示秀美风光,歌颂纯洁美丽的忠贞爱情,弘扬传统历史文化,打造七夕节庆品牌。

2. 桃花相亲会

每年三月,天河山景区都会举办"桃花相亲会",为广大待婚男女提供一个多彩的交友平台。爱情山上情谊浓,更有桃花相映红。阳春三月万物萌动,正是走出家门融入自然的最好时节,全国各地的游人来到天河山,沐浴春光,踏青越岭,登高抒怀,徜徉桃林花海,漫步九天银河,体验节会快乐,寻觅心仪之人。

交通路线:

1. 邢台以北城市:京珠高速(邢台段断交,邢台北下高速,邢台南上高速)—邢汾高速(路罗口下高速)—邢左公路(行驶19千米)—中国爱情山景区。

2. 邢台以南城市:京珠高速—邢汾高速(路罗口下高速)—邢左公路(行驶19千米)—中国爱情山景区。

Chapter Four

Characteristic Celebration Places of Double Seventh Festival

Meeting on the Magpie Bridge is a legendary love story. It is said that the Cowherd and the Weaving Maid meet on the Magpie Bridge on the seventh of the seventh lunar month. Therefore, Double Seventh Festival is also hailed as Chinese Valentine's Day. The beautiful story of the Cowherd and Weaving Maid is known as one of the four love tragedies in ancient Chinese literature, but its origin of circulation has not yet been determined.

1. Dongguan City, Guangdong Province: "Double Seventh Altars" in Wangniudun Town

The Skill Praying Festival in Wangniudun Town, Dongguan, Guangdong, well-known for its "Double Seventh Altars", has a long history, which originated from the Five Dynasties. With time passing, the festival has been enriched in content, but it still keeps its quaint charm. Wangniudun Town has been awarded the title "Hometown of Chinese Skill Praying Culture", and Double Seventh Cultural Festival has been put into the intangible cultural heritage list of Guangdong Province.

Wangniudun Double Seventh Cultural Festival comes from the love story between the Cowherd and the Weaving Maid, one of the four folk love stories passed on for thousands of years in China, hence having an extensive grassroots basis. Wangniudun aims to build itself into a famous town characteristic with Chinese Double Seventh Culture, and five sessions of Double Seventh Cultural Festival have been successfully held since 2004. Now Wangniudun Double Seventh Cultural Festival has a greater influence among the country owing to its increasing scale and special characteristics. After elaborate designing and preparation, Wangniudun Double Seventh Cultural Festival has developed from a small town activity into a nationally renowned cultural event, becoming a unique cultural symbol of the town and honored as the "The Festival of Mass Art, the Feast of Grassroots Culture".

Renowned Skill Praying Culture in Wangniudun

In 2010, Wangniudun Double Seventh Cultural Festival was listed into "Our Festivals" – the series of cultural activity

217

in Dongguan, and "The First Art Festival of Farmers" – the series of cultural activity hosted by China's Ministry of Culture and Ministry of Agriculture. "Double Seventh Altars" have been put on display in many major exhibitions, including: the First Exhibition of Intangible Cultural Heritage Protection in Guangdong, the Exchanging Meeting on Protecting and Inheriting Intangible Cultural Heritage held by Guangdong and ASEAN (Association of Southeast Asian Nations), and the Intangible Cultural Heritage Exhibition in "Guangdong Week" of Shanghai Expo. In 2010, the "Double Seventh Altar" entitled Destiny between Celestial Being and Human Being, was selected into the "Mountain Flower Award" in the 10th China Folk Literature.

Wangniudun "Double Seventh Altars" have already been collected into Guangdong Provincial Museum, Dongguan Exhibition Hall, Dongguan Intangible Cultural Heritage Protection Center and Dongguan Foods Customs Museum, bringing forth a wider inheritance and development of the Festival's artistic charm and social influence.

The Origin of the Name of Wangniudun Town

Wangniudun is a town famous for its traditional Chinese culture on Skill Praying, and it is the only town in Guangdong Province with the name containing the Chinese character "niu" (meaning "cattle"), which indicates a close link between the town and the love story on the Cowherd and the Weaving Maid. As for the origin of the town's name, there are two related versions of the story widespread in the folk.

One version of the story is narrated in the form of a legend. According to the account in Records of Wangniudun Town, Wangniudun, first built in the Song Dynasty, was originally a wide stretch of beach in the downstream of a tributary of East River, featuring fecund land, pleasant climate and lush grass. It was a good natural pasture that attracted the surrounding villagers to graze their cattle here. By the beach there was a raised mound, where trees grew and provided a shade for the villagers to take a rest. So the villagers often stood on the mound to watch over

The Performance "Dance of the Weaving Maid" in the Opening Ceremony of Wangniudun Double Seventh Cultural Festival

their cattle grazing. Hence the mound was named by villagers Wangniudun (meaning "a mound watching over the cattle"). As more and more villagers moved to live around the mound, the area belonging to the mound gradually expanded and evolved into today's Wangniudun Town.

The other version of the story is an interesting myth. Long time ago, on Double Seventh Day when the Cowherd should date with the Weaving Maid, the Queen Mother of the West secretly dispatched two heaven soldiers to prevent their dating. The two heaven soldiers transformed into a big tiger and a small one to chase and intercept the divine bull – the Cowherd's mount, but the valiant divine bull made every effort to fight

219

against the two tigers, managing to send the Cowherd and his two children to the Magpie Bridge on the Heaven River. In the fighting, the divine bull was unfortunately wounded and forced to run away down to the earth. When passing a mound with lush grass, the bull ran straight into it and disappeared. The two tigers at its heels had to stop and guard around the mound day and night. Later, the mound inhabited by the divine bull evolved into today's Wangniudun Town while the big and the small tigers became the Big Tiger Mountain and Small Tiger Mountain in the nearby Humen Town today.

Double Seventh Altars

With the approaching of Skill Praying Day every year, all twenty one villages in Wangniudun Town would be busy in preparing altars for the festival. So, the town would have been filled with festival atmosphere even before its arrival. Women are usually busy with preparing the offerings which will be put on the altars of ancestral hall in a beautiful manner. It is said that on the midnight of Skill Praying Day, the Weaving Maid, with her six elderly sisters, would come to the earth through the Magpie Bridge. And she would meet the Cowherd in the ancestral hall with the most beautiful altar. Various altars are put in the middle of ancestral halls, with seven teacups and seven different kinds of fruits on them. The fruits are heaped up like small hills. And the altars are surrounded by seven kinds of flowers, with a couple of big vases among them, inserted with beautiful branches of flowers. And ingenious women often weave a bridge of flowers with these branches. On the altar, there are a couple of red candles, and a golden censer is put on the center of it. Around the altar are seven red wooden chairs, with seven old-style clothes of different colors hanging on them. Next to each chair lays an ancient dressing table, where old-style dressing tools were orderly put, such as wooden comb, rouge, hairpin, etc. It will take from a week to months to make an altar for Double Seventh Day, and the process of preparation well shows the ingenuity of girls and young wives.

Wangniudun Double Seventh Cultural Festival Visited by Huge Crowds of People

There are mainly three forms of Double Seventh Altars in Wangniudun Town. The first form is the one prepared within a family: each household prepare a square table for the offering. The second is the one prepared with joined efforts of seven girls, who make an altar together, using from two to eight square tables. The third is the one prepared by the whole village: with fund raised in the village, the girls decorate ten more square tables covered with red clothes. They put on the tables such things as seven kinds of flowers, fruits, colorful ornaments, vivid dolls, etc. These girls wish to impress both gods and human with their exquisite handicrafts, so that they

221

could be blessed with happy love and marriages. The activities of Skill Praying are held only among the girls and young wives, while men and elderly women only watch standing by.

On Double Seventh Day, offerings like tea, wine, vegetarian meal and corns are placed on the altars to be savored by the seven fairies; also set out are handmade dragon, phoenix and lion that can be performed to celebrate the arrival of the festival; then seven kinds of flowers and fruits, seven pairs of embroidered shoes, seven sets of tables and chairs, and seven sets of clothes are presented to the seven fairies; last but not least, hand-made models of the Cowherd and the Weaving Maid are shown to replay the scene of meeting on the Magpie Bridge. Women try their best to display their ingenuity in handicrafts: plum blossom made by pistachio shell; chrysanthemum piled by white rice; lotus made by onion peel; lamps carved from egg shell; dragon column inlaid by wax gourd seeds; phoenix candle made by colorful wicks; butterflies over flowers made by clam shell powder; cherry blossom made by red melon seeds; small shoes embroidered by hands. All of these enrich the form and content of Skill Praying Festival, displaying the skill and beauty of folk handicraft completely.

"While the lovers reunite happily in heaven on Double Seventh Day,

People on earth worship the Altair and the Vega to pray for skill."

During the Skill Praying Festival, the ancestral halls in every villages of Wangniudun are packed with people, coming not only from Guangdong province, but also from other places home and abroad, all attracted by the reputation of Wangniudun cultural festival. The local activities of worship

Crowds Visiting the Double Seventh Altar

are held under traditional rituals: only maids and children are qualified for the ceremony – boys worship the Cowherd while girls worship the Weaving Maid. And the worship is performed by people one after another orderly, first the younger, then the elder. In the worshipping process, one should first have a sip of sugar water and wash his hands in the incense-soaked water, and then he should salute for three times and kowtow for nine times devoutly. After the ceremony, people would sit in the hall quietly to wait for the distributed presents, and the elders in the hall will give out the offerings on the altar to every worshiper. It's said that people will receive blessings from the Weaving Maid if they get the articles on the altar.

Wangniudun Double Seventh Cultural Festival

Every year around Double Seventh Day, there will be held a grand Cultural Festival on the square of Wangniudun Town.

From August 5th to 7th in 2015, the sixth Wangniudun Double Seventh Cultural Festival was held with the theme "Romantic Double Seventh Day, Happy Wangniudun Town". Focusing on the four keywords "romance, harmony, innovation and happiness", the Cultural Festival included seven major activities: opening ceremony party, cultural forum on Double Seventh Day, special exhibition of Double Seventh Altars, inspection of the priority project on constructing famous urban area for Double Seventh Festival, exhibition of cultural by-products from Double Seventh Festival, exhibition of records on previous Double Seventh Cultural Festivals, and exhibition of achievements on social economic development. On the very Double Seventh Day, over 100,000 tourists swarmed into Wangniudun, indulging in the wonderful cultural feast by appreciating altar exhibition, making vow, crossing the Magpie Bridge and watching wonderful performances. They personally experienced the wonderful charm and vitality of culture and art, enjoying its valve in art, business and society.

From August 8th to 10th in 2016, the Seventh Wangniudun Double Seventh Cultural Festival was held ceremoniously and attracted about 100,000 tourists to enjoy and participate once again. During the festival, there were all kinds of activities organized around three major themes: "Romantic Dating in Wangniudun", "Culture Exhibition of Folk Customs in Wangniudun", and "Showing Your Love in Happy Wangniudun ". These wonderful activities continued one after another, included: large-scale exhibition of Double Seventh Altars, longing for love – romantic dating, praying for love – releasing lotus lantern on the river, taste of love – 3D print of lovely snacks, feast of love – night praying on Double

Seventh Day, memory of love – the folk customs exhibition of waterside town, everlasting moment of love – collection of happy photos, melody of love – concert of classical love songs, and so on. The exhibition of "Double Seventh Altars" was still the main event of Double Seventh Cultural Festival in 2016. All twenty one villages of the town took part in the making and evaluating activities on "Double Seventh Altars", presenting a cultural feast to tourists by showing splendid views and exquisite workmanship of "Double Seventh Altars" in Wangniudun.

Travel Tips

Wangniudun: "The Hometown of Skill Praying Culture in China"

Wangniudun Town, located in the west of Dongguan city, Guangdong province, enjoys a history of over 800 years since it was first built in Song Dynasty. It gains the name "A Land Abounding in Fish and Rice" for its fecund land, pleasant climate and convenient transportation.

Wangniudun boasts convenient transportation and favorable geographic location, which is only 10km from the downtown area of Dongguan city, 40km from Guangzhou city and 90km from Shenzhen city. Meanwhile, the town has a bank line over 10km, which can hold in ships of two thousand tons, and it's only 5km from the Xinsha Port of Guangzhou and Humen Port of Dongguan, making it a newly developing waterside town.

Famous Spots of Sight:

Double Seventh Cultural Park; Experiencing Area of Wangniudun Dragon Boat Culture

Best Traveling Time:

April to June, August to November

Traffic Routes:

1. Start from Guangzhou Airport or Railway Station, and drive southward along Guangzhou–Shenzhen Expressway or Yanjiang Expressway for 40 km until you arrive at Wangniudun town.

2. Start from Shenzhen Bao'an Airport or Shenzhen Railway Station, and drive northwest along Guangzhou–Shenzhen Expressway or Yanjiang Expressway for 90 km until you arrive at Wangniudun town.

2. Yunxi County, Hubei Province: County of Double Seventh Culture, Love in the Heaven River (i.e. Tianhe River)

Yunxi County, at the junction between Hubei and He'nan, is located in the northwest border of Hubei Province. It is said to be the birthplace of Double Seventh Culture, because many of its places, attractions, legends and customs, are consistent with the story of Cowherd and the Weaving Maid.

On every year, if people look up at the starry sky, they will find a dazzling bright star in the east, which is the Star of Weaving Maid (i.e. Vega). Based on the experts' research, the seventh lunar month was ancient women's weaving time, so this star was called the Star of Weaving Maid. While in the eighth lunar month, ancient states would choose sacrifices of cattle, as a result of which the brightest star in that month was called the Star of Cowherd (i.e. Altair). On the stellar map, the vast galaxy is from north to south with Altair in the east and Vega in the west. The two stars are separated by the Milky Way, twinkling to each other. While in the center of Yunxi County, there is a serpentine Tianhe river flowing from north to south, originating from Shaanxi. And the geographical appearance around Tianhe corresponds with the astronomical layout curiously, with Yangs' River and Returning Fairy River to its east, and Beauty River and Fairy River to the west.

The Tianhe (meaning "Heaven River") in Yunxi not only coincides in name with the river in the story of the Cowherd and Weaving Maid, but also is linked closely with the natural and artificial landscapes in the river basin. In Tianhe basin, there is a stone on the mountain near Shimen Bay in southeast Yunxi County, which looks like a woman and is called "Stone Grandma"; while there is also a peak on Huagai Hill in the northwest, called "Stone Grandpa" for it looks like a man. All generations of local people think that the two mountain stones are the incarnations of the Cowherd and the Weaving Maid. In the upstream of Tianhe, there is a towering boulder called "Gold

The Opening Ceremony of Tianhe Double Seventh Cultural Festival

Hairpin Stone", said to be the incarnation of the gold hairpin that the Queen Mother left behind after she drew a river with her hairpin. In the Hanging Drum Park west of Yunxi County, there is a rock looking like a "suspended drum", which is said to be the stone left by Fairy Nvwa when she patched the sky, or a magic stone where the Weaving Maid placed her clothes when she bathed in the mortal world. And to the east of Tianhe, there stands the Queen Mother Hill with an elevation of 1069 meters, on the top of which there is the Queen Mother Temple with a statue of the Queen Mother worshipped.

On the Stone ladder Mountain northeast of the Hanging Drum Temple, there is a Heaven Pool Nunnery, which was frequently visited by worshipers long time ago. As the temple and the nunnery are opposite in position, and monks and nuns opposite in gender, it was proved that the two buildings were set up by honest Yunxi people to commemorate the Cowherd and the Weaving Maid.

Where there is Tianhe, there is the legend of the Cowherd and the Weaving Maid, and follows the unique folk customs of Double Seventh Festival. In Yunxi, people hand down the faithful love story about the Cowherd and the Weaving Maid from generation to generation. The elderly always advice the younger generation that: boys should be hardworking, rustic, kind and persistent like the Cowherd; girls should be clever, faithful, thrifty and filial like the Weaving Maid. Yunxi is the birthplace of beauties, and girls of Yunxi are well-known to be beautiful, kind, and skillful in hand. That's why there is a saying in the west of Hubei Province, "If you want to taste good rice, please go to Zhuxi; but if you want to take a good wife, please go to Yunxi." Experts believe that there exist the prototypes of the Cowherd and the Weaving Maid in reality, then they are evolved into the mythology.

In Tianhe basin of Yunxi, there are plenty widely-spread customs on Double Seventh Festival, such as skill praying by threading needles, skill divining by throwing needles onto water, birthday celebration of the cow, skill divining by watching spider's web, worshiping Kuixing (the God of Literacy), listening to whispers of love under the grape trellis, holding the lantern show for blessing, eating Skill Snacks and so forth. People celebrate Skill Praying Festival on the seventh of the seventh lunar month. On that day, women organize various handicraft competitions to improve their skills. When night falls, people come to the river to float lanterns, which express people's mourning for the lost beloved and blessing for the families, and serve as a guide for the Cowherd so that he could meet the Weaving Maid as soon as possible. "River lanterns are shining, river lanterns are bright; the Cowherd and the Weaving Maid meet in delight." The folk song is widely spread in Yunxi County.

In Yunxi, "Seven" is also a special number. In marriage customs there is a saying, "Seven is 'Yes' and eight is 'No'." When a man goes to a woman's home to propose marriage, the woman's family will entertain the man. If there are seven dishes at the dinner table, it means "Yes" to the proposal; while eight dishes represent "No". On the feast, when people make finger-guessing game over drinking, they would say the phrase "Seven Skills" to stand for the number "Seven". What's more, weddings and funerals are also associated with "Seven". While weddings have seven days off, funerals usually last for seven periods, each period consisting of seven days.

Folk ditties and mourning songs in Yunxi also contain many elements of the story on the Cowherd and the Weaving Maid. A complete folk song on the Cowherd and the Weaving Maid in Yunxi include the following stanzas: Giving a Wrong Imperial Edict, Cowherd Visiting the Garden, Weaving Maid Embroidering with Ten Needles, Meeting in the Garden, Degraded to the Mortal World, Sufferings of Cowherd, Brothers Living Apart, Weaving Maid's Yearning in Four Seasons, Weaving Maid Sneaking to the Mortal World, An Eventful Night for Cowherd, Old Cow Being a Matchmaker, Cowherd and Weaving Maid Watching Lanterns, Weaving Maid Pregnant, Harvest Tasting Festival in Autumn, Arresting Weaving Maid, Meeting on Magpie Bridge, and so forth.

In recent years, Yunxi County has implemented the strategy of "Developing the County by Tourism", trying its best to build a town of Double Seventh Culture centering on the area of Tianhe. The town aims to be an excellent Chinese tourist attraction adapt to different needs: wedding, dating and entertaining. On the infrastructure construction, Yunxi has built two national 4-A level scenic areas: Wulong River and Longtan River, which are respectively compared to mini versions of two famous Chinese scenic areas: Jiuzhaigou and Yandang. And now, Yunxi is planning the construction of Tianhe Scenic Area, Estuary Ancient Town and World Wedding Custom Expo Park. Now a series of Double Seventh cultural projects have been finished, including Tianhe Folk Custom Museum, Tianhe Square, Double Seventh Square, Double Seventh Cultural Park, Tianhe International Hotel, etc.

Meanwhile, Yunxi County has successfully held China (Yunxi) – Tianhe Double Seventh Cultural Festival for six consecutive times. Around Double Seventh Festival every year, a series of activities are organized and publicized continuously through the mainstream media, for example, selecting the Tianhe Image Ambassador of Weaving Maid, recruiting couples for the Wedding Ceremony for, collecting Double Seventh cultural songs in Tianhe Yunxi, seminar of Double Seventh Culture, wedding ceremony "Witnessed by Tianhe", special theatrical performances, guests' cruise for Wulong River and so on. These activities have spread widely Double Seventh Culture in Yunxi, increasing greatly the influence and popularity of Yunxi Double Seventh cultural tourism. At the same time, Double Seventh Culture gradually infiltrates into every aspect of life in Yunxi, which can be shown by the names of many municipal projects, roads and bridges, buildings and landscapes under construction, all given by the government to echo Tianhe Double Seventh Culture. Besides, Enterprises register trademarks, give trade names, replace doorplates, and change business names, reflecting Double Seventh Culture as well. As a result, elements of Tianhe Double Seventh Culture are found in every corner of Yunxi, nourishing local people's mind and soul, affecting their way of life and convention, and becoming the cultural consciousness down into the bone and blood of Yunxi people.

Travel Tips

Yunxi County, Hubei Province

Yunxi county features its long cultural tradition, rich travelling resources, beautiful natural scenery and diverse ecological species. With profound cultural background, Yunxi is considered the Chinese hometown of Double Seventh Culture, of magpies and of tung trees. It is also the national aromatic tobacco base and one of "four national eucommia base". In recent years, Yunxi has built places such as Wulong River, Longtan River, Shangjin Ancient Town and Tianhe into national 4–A level scenic areas, and opened 150 more hotels and restaurants, 400 more shops of tourism products, with more than fifty kinds of famous tourism products for sale, including products of such brands as "Weaving Maid", "Double Seventh", and "Heaven River".

As an important originating and inheriting place of Double Seventh Culture, Yunxi has carried out forcefully the strategy of "Building the County into An Attraction" in urban construction, aiming to set up a county featuring Double Seventh Culture with good ecological environment, suitable for living, working and travelling. There are ten cultural squares and entertainment parks like Double Seventh Square, Tianhe Square, and Double Seventh Cultural Stories Park. Such landscapes built on Double Seventh Square as the time tunnel, the greatest bronze cow of the world, the man–made moon and the music fountain, form a "Grand View Garden of Double Seventh Culture". Twelve "Spring Bridges" are set up with special flavor of Double Seventh Culture, including "New Spring Bridge", "Expecting Spring Bridge", "Welcoming Spring Bridge", etc. Also there is a Tianhe Water Landscape under construction, and roads are named as "Double Seventh Road", "Tianhe Road"... Urban roads, bridges, gardens, squares, hills and rivers, all these contain elements of Double Seventh Culture, which has deeply penetrated into the "skin" and "blood" of Yunxi.

In addition to elements of Double Seventh Culture dotted everywhere, you could see the prosperity of Double Seventh Industry while walking in Yunxi county, represented by "Tianhe" silk quilts "Weaving Maid" walnut oil, Double Seventh Hotel, etc··· At night, thousands of local residents would gather on the Tianhe Square, enjoying themselves by dancing, playing badminton, skating and so on.

Famous Spots of Sight:

Wulong River Scenic Area; Longtan River Scenic Area; Double Seventh Tianhe Square; Shangjin Ancient Town

Best Traveling Time:

May to October

Traffic Routes:

1. Road traffic: You can choose Fuzhou – Yinchuan Expressway (G70). There are about 240km from Xi'an city of Shaanxi province to Yunxi, and about 70km from Shiyan city of Hubei province to Yunxi.

2. Air traffic: The nearest airport is Wudangshan Airport in Shiyan city, which is 80km from Yunxi, about an hour's car ride.

3. Lianshan County, Guangdong Province: "Sweet Seventh Month" Zhuang Water Playing Festival

Lianshan Zhuang-Yao Autonomous County is located in the northwest of Guangdong Province, at the border region of Guangdong, Hunan and Guangxi provinces. It is 300 kilometers west to Guilin and 265 kilometers south to Guangzhou.

It is said that on the seventh of the seventh lunar month, the seven fairies in the sky would bath in the Heaven River for fun. And around noon, water from the Heaven River would flow into streams and rivers on earth, so the river of Zhuang nationality would become particularly cool and clean, which would be very beneficial for the health of human body. Bathing in the river this day can remove disasters, eliminate toxins, exorcise evils, beautify the bodies, avoid illness and prolong lives. Therefore, whenever the day comes, Zhuang people, regardless of sex or age, would gather in the river to wash hair, bath and play with water, longing for health and longevity,

The Terraces of Zhuang People in Lianshan County

peace and good luck. If water of this day is used to make vinegar, its smell would be mellow and last long. That's why the day is also called "Sweet Seventh Month", "Girls' Day", and "Long Lasting Day".

Zhuang Nationality in Lianshan has kept this custom for thousands of years, which evolves into a grand festival of the Zhuang Nationality – "Sweet Seventh Month" Zhuang Water Playing Festival. The festival has been held on every Double Seventh Day since 2006, and lots of dormant traditional culture of Zhuang nationality are presented to the world once again. The Water Playing Festival is celebrated in various interactive performing areas, and programs presented to the tourists include: live performances of aboriginal songs and dances, exhibitions of national and provincial Intangible Cultural Heritage, folk crafts of ethnic groups, custom performances of Zhuang and Yao nationalities, water playing carnival, flavor foods of Zhuang and Yao nationalities.

Opening Ceremony of "Sweet Seventh Month" Zhuang Water Playing Festival

First, visitors are welcomed by the gallery which is 50 meters long and full of ethnic flavors of Zhuang and Yao nationalities. Red carpets are put on the Zhuang-Yao-flavor bridge on Shangji Road, Jishui County, and Zhuang-Yao-flavor pictures are hanging on both sides of the corridor. Banners with Zhuang anb Yao totems flutter and rustle in the wind. Beautiful Zhuang girls in holiday array welcome guests comeing from afar by putting on Zhang-style embroidered balls for them. At that moment, with Zhuang eight-instrument music playing, girls singing hvely songs politely lead guests to their seats just opposite to the water playing stage.

Second, ethnic arts and crafts on both sides of the river catch people's eyes fast. At the water playing passageways on both sides of the river, there are shows of Yao small-long-drum dance (which is a national intangible cultural heritage) and Yao eight-instrument music (which is a provincial intangible cultural heritage). A lot of cultural art events dispersing in different festivals and places are all acted out on the stage of this festival. A 1000-meter-long street condenses a 1000-year-long cultural tradition of Zhuang and Yao nationalities, where arts and crafts are so abundant in forms that they cannot be appreciated at one sitting.

Third, people worship the water god for blessings and splash around in the river. On the stage in the middle of the river, with the sounds of drums rising from slow to fast and from faint to strong, a team holding serrated-edged triangular flags rushes up from two side stages, and a Zhuang wizard walks onto the main stage reciting sacrificial words and shaking copper bells, to worship the water god solemnly. Then aboriginal songs and dances start: folk song of Zhuang nationality *Guests Visit Our Hometown* welcomes guests from all directions; merry music of *Water Playing Song and Dance* inspires the desires of both Zhuang youths and guests on riversides to splash around in water. As soon as the show is

"Sweet Seventh Month" Zhuang Water Playing Festival in Lianshan, Guangdong

over, 400 boys and girls in Zhuang ethnic array jump into the river, splashing water over each other and singing songs happily. Thousands of guests successively walks into the river and join the water revelry.

Fourth, Palatable Zhuang-Yao-flavor foods arouse the visitors' appetites successfully. A great number of specialties hidden in Zhuang folk are presented to the public during the festival: delicious glutinous rice cake, mouthwatering "Baisan" bacon, luscious steamed stuffed bun wrapped in lotus leaf.... Hotels, restaurants and snack bars also welcome guests by selling signature dishes of local flavor. Apart from enjoying a sumptuous feast at the gourmet festival, tourists can purchase some unprocessed food materials at the street of local specialties and bring them home for future savoring.

After an exhausting day of celebration, it is most pleasant for tourists to taste some local-flavored snacks and Yao-style

Lianshan Yao and Zhuang Autonomous County Featuring Strong Flavors of Yao and Zhuang Ethnic Cultures

237

Ethnic Customs Performance on the Opening Ceremony of Lianshan Zhuang Water Playing Festival

glutinous rice wine at the riversides with refreshing breeze blowing gently. The next day, there are plenty of new scenic spots waiting for them to visit, such as "Yaoshan Waterfall", "Jinzi Sun-watching Platform" "Yingyang Strategic Pass" and so on.

Travel Tips

Lianshan Zhuang-Yao Autonomous County

The county's total population is nearly 120,000, 63% of which are Zhuang, Yao and other ethnic minorities. In China, it is the only Zhuang-Yao Autonomous County, having successfully held "Sweet Seventh

Month" – Zhuang Water Playing Festival for years. No wonder that its Zhuang–Yao custom tourism crown the southern area of Guangdong.

Spots of Sight:

The tourist resources in Lianshan are abundant. There is Daxushan Waterfall Tourist Area (nicknamed "Jiuzhaigou in Guangdong"), Yingyangguan scenic spot (bordering three provinces), beautiful Boundary River between Guangdong and Guangxi Provinces, quaint Fulin Garden, Gold Tour (blending water–playing and physical exercise perfectly), splendid Maotian Cloud Sea, and so forth. Besides, as a minority–compact community, Lianshan has its own special cultural tradition, including beating gongs on the Spring Festival, snatching gongs and firecrackers for good luck, launching sky lanterns and so on. Zhuang people's architectures, festivals and marriage customs are all endowed with distinctive ethnic characteristics.

Best Traveling Time:

November to February

Traffic Routes:

1. 323 National Highway. It runs through the whole area of Lianshan, connecting Shaoguan city of Guangdong Province in the east, and Hezhou and Liuzhou cities of Guangxi Zhuang autonomous region in the west.

2. G55 Expressway. The Guangdong line of Erenhot–Guangzhou Expressway was opened to traffic On December 31, 2014. It connects Hu'nan, Guangxi, and Guangdong provinces, convenient for one to drive from Guangzhou city, Shenzhen city or Changsha city to Lianshan.

3. Air traffic. The nearest airport is Baiyun Airport in Guangzhou city. It is two hours' car ride from Lianshan to Baiyun Airport by taking Erenhot–Guangzhou Expressway.

4. The Tianhe Mountain, Hebei Province: Double Seventh Lovers' Festival

Xingtai is the nationally-recognized cradle and research

centre of Chinese Double Seventh Culture. Situated deep in the Taihang Mountain, the Tianhe Mountain Scenic Spot registered as "China's Love Mountain" in 2005 under the permission of the State Administration of Industry and Commerce, because it is the birthplace of the famous love story on the Cowherd and the Weaving Maid, and is endowed with abundant cultural relics and popular legends.

Since August, 2006, Double Seventh Lovers' Festival has been held around Double Seventh Day annually in Hebei for 11 years. And acclaimed twice by the authority as a star Chinese traditional festival in 2007 and 2010, it has become a new cultural brand of Hebei Province, making beneficial attempts to foster a nationwide festival of distinct Chinese features and to publicize traditional Chinese culture. Since its birth, Double Seventh Lovers' Festival has all along been co-hosted by the Committee Office for Building Spiritual Civilization of Hebei Province, the Publicity Department of Xingtai Municipal Committee and the Tianhe Mountain Scenic Spot in Xingtai City.

In 2015, a host of activities of "Double Seventh Lovers' Festival" were held at the Tianhe Mountain Scenic Spot. For instance, on Aug. 15th, "Love 1+1" FM896 Blind Date Party, thrown by the virtue of radio, was attended by ten thousand single youths within and without Hebei province; on Aug. 20th, a performance of local folk customs was staged, together with exhibitions of Xingtai folk handicraft and textile products; from Aug. 15th to Aug. 20th, a show characterized with folk land-and-water marital customs was performed with the theme "Reviewing Classics, Saluting Love"; and from Aug. 20th to Aug. 22th, Yanjing Beer Music Festival was held to present a super fun Double Seventh Festival. These events show the history and development of China's love culture to tourists and involve them into a unique Double Seventh Festival.

Double Seventh Lovers' Festival held in 2016 contains five major activities, including "Looking for Contemporary Weaving Maids", "Works on the Theme of Love and Marriage", "Theme Song Concert", "Experience-Exchanging Conference by Contemporary Weaving Maids" and "High-Level Forum of Double Seventh Culture". Among them, "Looking for Contemporary Weaving Maids" aims at investigating and electing women with skills, talents, filial piety and kind hearts at the grass-roots level, and to attend the activity one can register through the internet or be qualified by the recommendation of her working unit. Double Seventh Festival is originally observed in honor of working women, and the Weaving Maid is considered as their representative for

Modern Women in the Contest of Threading Needle for Skill Praying

Chinese Love Festival at the Foot of the Great Wall, Shanhaiguan Pass

being diligent, beautiful, virtuous, plain, wise, brave and etc. The Weaving Maid and the Cowherd worked hard in their own position, and their cooperation and diligence created a life full of love, harmony and happiness. Thus, "Looking for Contemporary Weaving Maids" means to find out excellent women in our modern society, publicize their impressive achievements, support their work, and encourage more women to be strong and independent so that they can devote themselves to the construction of an even better-off society.

Every year during the festival, the grand occasion of "Ten Thousand People Celebrating Together" often comes into being. Some special activities are held at the same time, like the performance of folk land-and-water marital customs, the meeting of ten thousand people on the Magpie Bridge, the performance of Xingtai folk customs, and exhibitions for handicraft and textile products. Moreover, there are exhibitions of "intangible cultural heritage" folk cultures from Beijing, Tianjin and Hebei, presenting a colorful landscape of folk culture to the public. The exhibition of traditional folk arts and crafts combines various products with ancient love story, so that visitors can have a more comprehensive understanding of the beautiful love story between the Cowherd and the Weaving Maid.

The performance of traditional marriage customs is also a highlight of Double Seventh Lovers' Festival, not only offering a feast to visitors' eyes, but also prompting people to understand better traditional love culture. The activity invites experts to verify data and research deeply, and organize the staff of scenic area to reprogram the performance on the folk land-and-water marital customs in the Han Dynasty, aiming to show the visitors authentic ancient love culture. In the activities of former years, the organizers also selected "Loving Couples from Harmonious Families", whose exemplary roles received positive responses from the general public.

Travel Tips

Tianhe Mountain: China's Love Mountain

Located in Xingtai City, Hebei Province, Tianhe Mountain area is considered the hometown of Chinese Double Seventh Culture and the native habitat of the legend on the Cowherd and the Weaving Maid. It is the greenest part of the Taihang Mountains, which lie in the border of Shanxi province and Hebei province, and it is 50 kilometres away from Xingtai city with a total area of 30 square kilometres. Here is the famous "Watery Town of Taihang Mountains" , with its wonderful peaks, deep valleys, lush vegetation, cascading waterfalls, babbling springs and abundant water resources. It is also known as "The Grassland on Top of Clouds" for the wind symphony in the pines and large herds of sheep and cows.

The Tianhe Mountain Scenic Area has been rated as national 4−A level scenic area, national key scenic spot and national geological park. When people set foot on this land, it is just like being in a wonderland. Tianhe Mountain is especially renowned for its waters. It is known that every five step appears a waterfall and every ten step a pool.

Traffic Routes:

Beijing−Zhuhai Expressway—Xingtai−Fenyang Expressway (drive off in Luluokou)—Xingtai−Zuoquan Highway (drive for 19 kilometres)—the Tianhe Mountain Scenic Area.

Cultural Activities:

1. Love Cultural Festival

Every year during Double Seventh Festival, "Love Cultural Festival" would be held in the Tianhe Mountain Scenic Area. Based on the legend of the Weaving Maid and the Cowherd, "Tianhe Mountain Love Cultural Festival" aims to show the splendid scenery of Taihang Mountain, eulogize wonderful true love, promote traditional historic culture, build up the celebration brand of Double Seventh Festival.

2. Blind Date around the Peach Blossom

Every March, "Blind Date around the Peach Blossom" would be organized at the Tianhe Mountain Scenic Area to provide a wonderful dating platform for singles. It is so romantic for them to meet at Tianhe Mountain while rosy peach blossoms are in bloom. With nature waking up, the lively March is the best season for people to go out into nature. People can go climbing and sightseeing in the joyful spring, enjoy the forest of peach blossoms, walk under the stars at night, experience the happy festival and find their Mr. or Mrs. Right.

结　语

　　七夕这个节日从先秦到现代,已经有几千年的历史了。历经几千年风雨的洗礼,七夕这一节日不断变化发展,形成了能够满足民众生理和心理需求的传统节日,调节着人与人、人与社会、人与自然万物间的种种关系,是不可替代的宝贵精神财富。

　　七夕节得以延续几千年的主要原因有三:一是只要人们看到银河,就会联想到牛郎织女这个美丽的传说故事。七夕正值夏末秋初之时,白天巧云布天,夜晚星光灿烂,是人们在户外观天的好时节。近年来,由于城市化加速,街区照明亮度大,影响了观天的效果,但是,随着社会的进步,人们终究要追求"回归自然",七夕到户外观天,不失为既回归传统又契合当下节日的"时尚"的节日活动。七夕由于和天象联系在一起,便具有了长久的生命力。二是七夕歌颂的是夫妻恩爱,和谐稳定。只要有家庭存在,夫妻白头偕老就是人生幸福的一大追求。社会竞争越激烈,夫妻之间的相互理解和支持就越重要,现在讲银婚、金婚、钻石婚等等,都是对夫妻生活的赞美。七夕的文化内涵与社会生活联系如此紧密,人们需要有一个展示夫妻情感和他人为其进行祝福的机会,所以七夕在当代更具时尚性。三是传统节日是中华文化的有效载体,中华振兴必然要表现在文化的繁荣上。七夕这个节日极具综合性和独特性,是中华节庆文化的重要代表,也是每年节庆周期链条中的重要一环,有了它才使得节庆文化丰富多彩,失去它就失去了节庆文化的完整性,所以它不会被人们忘记。

在城市化、信息化快速发展的今天，生活节奏加快，传统节庆赖以延续的条件发生了较大变化，七夕节的文化传承出现了一些困局。可喜的是，在2006年"七夕节"被列入中国国家级非物质文化遗产名录之后，原本沉寂的传统节日重新回到人们的视线中，特别是年轻一代正逐渐加深对"七夕节"内涵的认知，中国式的过节方式趋于流行。

传统节日历史悠久，中华文化博大精深，有着极为丰富的内涵，它期待着年轻一代去发掘，去继承，去弘扬。中国的七夕完全可以仿古塑今，传承和创新并行不悖，使几千年的文化习俗重拾辉煌，成为中国节日的主流。

Conclusion

Stretching back to the Pre-Qin period, Double Seventh Festival has a history of several thousand years. Due to historical and social reasons, it has experienced the vicissitudes in the long time, changing and developing constantly into a festival that can satisfy people's physical and mental needs. Coordinating myriads of relationships between man and man, man and society, and man and nature, Double Seventh Festival is indeed an irreplaceable and precious cultural legacy for human being.

The eternity of the festival originates from the following facts.

First, on seeing the Milky Way, people will think of the beautiful legend of the Cowherd and the Weaving Maid. Double Seventh Day comes at the time of late summer and early autumn, a good season for people to observe the sky with clouds at daytime and stars at night. In the recent years, sky observation has been deterred owing to accelerating urbanization and strengthening street lighting, but people will eventually return to nature with time going. Hence, going out for sky observation will come to vogue on Double Seventh Festival, which possesses long-lasting vitality for its association with celestial phenomena.

Second, Double Seventh Festival values conjugal love, harmony and stability. As long as family exists, the pursuit for happy marriage will never die. Nowadays the mutual understanding and support between couples is more and more important in this society featuring ever fiercer competition. Hence, people pay more attention to anniversaries such as "Silver Wedding", "Gold Wedding", "Diamond Wedding", etc. The cultural connotation of Double Seventh Festival is related closely to modern life, and it provides an opportunity for people to show their own conjugal love to others and to get blessing from others in return. That's why Double Seventh Festival is becoming increasingly popular in modern society.

Third, traditional festivals are effective carriers of Chinese culture and the revitalization of China is necessarily manifested by cultural prosperity. The comprehensiveness and uniqueness of Double Seventh Festival makes it an indispensable part of all festivals in China, without which the festive culture would be colorless and incomplete. Consequently, it would be etched in people's mind permanently.

The speedy urbanization, information explosion and accelerating pace of life has changed the celebrating surrounding of traditional festivals, so we are now encountering some hindrance in inheriting and promoting Double Seventh Culture. Much to our delight, however, the fading Double Seventh Festival has come back to the spotlight after being included in the national intangible cultural heritage list in 2006. Moreover, the traditional way of celebrating festival is turning popular now as the younger generation acquires a deeper understanding on the connotation of Double Seventh Festival.

The time-honored traditional festival, teeming with the rich and profound culture handed down from our forefathers, is there for the younger generations to explore, to inherit and to promote. As innovation and inheritance often go hand in hand, we surely can reshape today by learning from yesterday, make the ageold Double Seventh Festival glow with new radiance and stand out as one of the leading Chinese festivals.

七夕"巧果"的制作方法

Recipe for "Skill Snacks" of Double Seventh Festival

七夕节，又名乞巧节，起源于对自然的崇拜及妇女穿针乞巧，后被赋予牛郎织女的传说，使其成为象征爱情的节日。

"巧果"即"七夕果"，如同端午节吃粽子、中秋节吃月饼一样，七夕节这一天要吃"巧食"。"巧果"又名"乞巧果子""巧饼"，是用油、面、糖等做成的各种形状的小面点，香甜可口，是七夕节这天必做、必吃的一种传统节日面食。

Double Seventh Festival, also named Skill Praying Festival, comes from people's worship for nature, keeping the tradition that women pray for skills by threading needles, and symbolizing faithful love for the legendary story of the Cowherd and the Weaving Maid.

"Skill Snacks" or "Double Seventh Snacks", is a typical kind of food for Double Seventh Festival, just like zongzi for Double Fifth Festival, or mooncake for Mid-Autumn Festival. "Skill Snacks", also called "Skill Praying Snacks", "Skill Pastry", are sweet and delicious snacks of various shapes made from oil, flour, sugar and other ingredients. The traditional wheaten food is a must for Double Seventh Festival.

原料：
1. 面粉：500 克
2. 温水：220 克
3. 奶粉：15 克
4. 白糖：50 克
5. 酵母：1 小勺

Ingredients:
1. flour: 500g
2. warm water: 220g
3. milk powder: 15g
4. white sugar: 50g
5. yeast powder: a small spoonful

制作步骤 / Procedures

1. 温水溶解酵母，将酵母水分多次倒入掺有奶粉和白糖的面粉中。
1. Dissolve yeast powder in warm water, and pour in several times the yeast solution into the flour mixed with milk powder and white sugar.

2. 将面粉揉成均匀的面团，盖上保鲜膜，室温醒发 1 小时。醒发好的面团拿出来用手揉匀。面揉得时间越长，做出的成品越好吃，颜色越白。

2. Knead the flour into a smooth dough, cover it with plastic wrap, and let it rise for one hour at room temperature. Then take out the dough to knead. And the longer you knead the dough, the fairer and more delicious the knacks would be.

3. 把面团用模子压成型，烤盘铺好烤纸，将出模的面团摆入烤盘。

3. Divide the dough to small ones, press them into various shapes with molds, and put them onto the baking pan lined with baking paper.

253

4. 烤箱预热 185 度，烤 10 分钟即可。

4. Preheat the oven to 185 C°, and bake for 10 minutes.

丛书后记

　　上下五千年的悠久历史孕育了灿烂辉煌的中华文化。我国地域辽阔，民族众多，节庆活动丰富多彩，而如此众多的节庆活动就是一座座珍贵丰富的旅游资源宝藏。在中华民族漫长的历史长河中，春节、清明、端午、中秋等传统节日和少数民族节日，是中华民族优秀传统文化的历史积淀，是中华民族精神和情感传承的重要载体，是维系祖国统一、民族团结、文化认同、社会和谐的精神纽带，是中华民族生生不息的不竭动力。

　　春节以正月为岁首，贴门神、朝贺礼；元宵节张灯、观灯；清明节扫墓、踏青、郊游、赏牡丹；端午节赛龙舟、包粽子；上巳节被禊；七夕节乞巧，牛郎会织女；中秋节赏月、食月饼；节日间的皮影戏、长安鼓乐；少数民族的节日赶圩、歌舞美食……这一桩桩有趣的节日习俗，是联络华人、华侨亲情、乡情、民族情的纽带，是中国非物质文化遗产的"活化石"。

　　为了传播中华民族优秀传统文化，推进中外文化交流，中国人类学民族学研究会民族节庆专业委员会与安徽人民出版社合作，继成功出版《中国节庆文化》丛书之后，再次推出《多彩中国节》丛书。为此，民族节庆专委会专门成立了编纂委员会，邀请了国际节庆协会（IFEA）主席兼首席执行官史蒂文·施迈德先生、中国文联原执行副主席冯骥才先生、第十一届全国政协民族和宗教委员会副主任周明甫先生等担任顾问，由《中外节庆网》总编辑彭新良博士担任主编，16 位知名学者组成编委会，负责

255

丛书的组织策划、选题确定、体例拟定和作者的甄选。

　　出版《多彩中国节》丛书，是民族节庆专业委员会和安徽人民出版社合作的结晶。安徽人民出版社是安徽省最早的出版社，有60余年的建社历史，在对外传播方面走在全国出版社的前列；民族节庆专业委员会是我国节庆研究领域唯一的国家级社团，拥有丰富的专家资源和地方节庆资源。这套丛书的出版，实现了双方优势资源的整合。丛书的面世，若能对推动中国文化的对外传播、促进传统民族文化的传承与保护、展示中华民族的文化魅力、塑造节庆的品牌与形象有所裨益，我们将甚感欣慰。

　　掩卷沉思，这套丛书凝聚着诸位作者的智慧，倾注着编纂者的心血，也诠释着中华民族文化的灿烂与辉煌。在此，真诚感谢各位编委会成员、丛书作者、译者以及出版社工作人员付出的辛劳，以及各界朋友对丛书编纂工作的鼎力支持！希望各位读者对丛书多提宝贵意见，以便我们进一步完善后续作品，将更加璀璨的节庆文化呈现在世界面前。

　　为了向中外读者更加形象地展示各民族的节庆文化，本丛书选用了大量图片。这些图片，既有来自于丛书作者的亲自拍摄，也有的来自于民族节庆专委会图片库（由各地方节庆组织、节庆主办单位报送并授权使用），还有部分图片是由编委会从专业图片库购买，或从新闻媒体中转载。由于时间关系，无法与原作者一一取得联系，请有关作者与本书编委会联系（邮箱：pxl@jieqing365.com），我们将按相关规定支付稿酬。特此致谢。

《多彩中国节》丛书编委会

2018年3月

Series Postscript

China has developed its splendid and profound culture during its long history of 5000 years. It has a vast territory, numerous nationalities as well as the colorful festivals. The rich festival activities have become the invaluable tourism resources. The traditional festivals, such as the Spring Festival, the Tomb-Sweeping Festival, the Dragon Boat Festival, the Mid-Autumn Festival as well as the festivals of ethnic minorities, represent the excellent traditional culture of China and have become an important carrier bearing the spirits and emotions of Chinese people, a spirit tie for the national reunification, national unity, cultural identity and social harmony, and an inexhaustible motive force for the development of Chinese nation.

The Spring Festival starts with Chinese lunar January, when people post pictures of the Door Gods and exchange gifts and wishes cheerfully. At the Lantern Festival a splendid light show is to be held and enjoyed. On the Tomb-Sweeping Festival, men and women will worship their ancestors by sweeping the tombs, going for a walk in the country and watching the peony. And then the Dragon Boat Festival witnesses a wonderful boat race and the making of zongzi. Equally interesting is the needling celebration on the Double Seventh Festival related to a touching love story of a cowboy and his fairy bride. While the Mid-Autumn Festival is characterized by moon-cake eating and moon watching. Besides all these, people can also enjoy shadow puppet shows, Chang'an

257

drum performance, along with celebration fairs, songs and dances and delicious snacks for ethic groups. A variety of festival entertainment and celebrations have formed a bond among all Chinese, at home or abroad, and they are regarded as the "living fossil" of Chinese intangible cultural heritage.

In order to spread the excellent traditional culture of China, and promote the folk festival brand for our country, the Folk Festival Commission of the China Union of Anthropological and Ethnological Science (CUAES) has worked with the Anhui People's Publishing House to publish *The Colorful Chinese Festivals Series*. For this purpose, the Folk Festival Commission has established the editorial board of *The Colorful Chinese Festivals Series*, by inviting Mr. Steven Wood Schmader, president and CEO of the International Festival And Events Association (IFEA); Mr. Feng Jicai, former executive vice-president of China Federation of Literary and Art Circles(CFLAC); Mr. Zhou Mingfu, deputy director of the Eleventh National and Religious Committee of the CPPCC as consultants; Dr. Peng Xinliang, editor-in-chief of the Chinese and foreign Festival Website as the chief editor; and 16 famous scholars as the members to organize, plan, select and determine the topics and the authors.

This series is the product of the cooperation between the Folk Festival Commission and Anhui People's Publishing House. Anhui People's Publishing House is the first publishing house in Anhui Province, which has a history of over 60 years, and has been in the leading position in terms of foreign transmission. The Folk Festival Commission is the only organization of national level in the field of research of the Chinese festivals, which has experts and rich local festival resources. The series has integrated the advantageous resources of both parties. We will be delighted and gratified to see that the series could promote the foreign transmission of the Chinese culture, promote the inheritance and preservation of the traditional and folk cultures, express the cultural charms of China and build the festival brand and image of China.

The Colorful Chinese Festivals Series is bearing the wisdoms and knowledge of all of its authors and the great efforts of the editors, and explaining the splendid cultures of the Chinese nation. We hereby sincerely express our gratitude to the members of the board, the authors, the translators and the personnel in the publishing house for their great efforts and to all friends from all walks of the society for their supports. We hope you can provide your invaluable opinions for us to further promote the following works so as to show the world our excellent festival culture.

This series uses a large number of pictures in order to unfold the festive cultures in a vivid way to readers at home and abroad. Some of them are shot by the authors themselves, some of them come from the picture database of the Folk Festival Commission (contributed and authorized by the local folk festival organizations or organizers of local festival celebrations), and some of them are bought from Saitu Website or taken from the news media. Because of the limit of time, we can't contact the contributors one by one. Please don't hesitate about contacting the editorial board of this series (e-mail: pxl@ jieqing365.com) if you're the contributor. We'll pay you by conforming to the state stipulations.

Editorial Committee of *The Colorful Chinese Festivals Series*
March, 2018